How Television
Invented New Media

How Television
Invented New Media

SHEILA C. MURPHY

RUTGERS UNIVERSITY PRESS
New Brunswick, New Jersey, and London

Library of Congress Cataloging-in-Publication Data

Murphy, Sheila C., 1974–.
  How television invented new media / Sheila C. Murphy.
      p.   cm.
  Includes bibliographical references and index.
  ISBN 978–0–8135–5004–6 (hardcover : alk. paper) —
ISBN 978–0–8135–5005–3 (pbk. : alk. paper)
      1. Television broadcasting—Technological innovations.
  2. Television—Technological innovations.   3. Interactive
television.   4. Convergence (Telecommunication)   5. Television
interactive toys.   I. Title.
      PN1992.5.M87 2011
      384.55—dc22
                                                              2010035282

  British Cataloging-in-Publication data for this book is available
              from the British Library.

Copyright © 2011 by Sheila C. Murphy

Visit our Web site: http://rutgerspress.rutgers.edu

Manufactured in the United States of America

For my mom, Margaret Anne Murphy (1947–2007),
and for Anne Friedberg (1952–2009), my hero and friend

CONTENTS

Acknowledgments

OFTEN, WHAT HAS GOTTEN ME THROUGH the more doubt-ridden and traumatic days of writing has been the idea that I might be able to dedicate this book to someone whose presence in my life helped shaped me and, by extension, what I do. Such dedications connect our navel-gazing academic efforts up to another set of conversations and exchanges that are deeply lived and felt. There is an accustomed rhythm and even academic industry standards for the dedication and acknowledgments section: institutions and colleagues in the beginning, family and friends at the end.[1] This is a format I plan to mess with just a bit here.

Yet in writing this dedication I found a lump in my throat and sentiments that were harder to fit into words than I expected when I began this project. I have been beyond fortunate to have the people in my life who I have met and counted on along the way. They made it possible in ways that are innumerable and varied for me to write this book. I have a chronic medical condition, and without such help I would never be, let alone write. Friends are the people who sit with you and pore over your work with coffee in hand, who support you through the days when, like Charlie Brown, you alone seem to have a rain cloud over your head, who share in your victories both big and small. Friends—and family—are dear. They go first. This book is dedicated to two such amazing friends—and family—of mine. During the extended period in which I wrote and researched this project I had the support of—and I lost—two of my dearest friends, mentors, and role models. They were my mother, Margaret Anne Murphy, and my mentor, Anne Friedberg.

When I was a young girl my mom was the most courageous person I knew. She worked tirelessly, she was creative, she was funny—snarky, with a dark sense of humor and an ability to cuss up a storm. She was supportive—at each figure-skating competition, science fair, hockey game, and soccer match. She died too young, too soon, a victim of the institutional inequalities that are routinely part of being the working poor in America. I was and still am proud to have been my mother's daughter and close friend. More often than not, I now hear her voice through mine, as I talk to students, as I write, as I am. She was tenacious and yet kind—both things I still finding myself striving to be.

Let me tell you a secret: I chose my graduate program exactly the way you are not supposed to choose it. I chose to attend the University of California, Irvine, so I could work with Anne Friedberg, a woman whom I knew only through her writing. Since our first meeting back in 1997, Anne was much more than an advisor to me. She was a trusted friend and, I'm proud to say, she was my colleague, too. We spent the better part of the 1990s and 2000s on her "espirt d'freeway" mobile phone calls, discussing theory, films, computers, art, and much, much more as she drove between Orange County and Los Angeles. She took me into her family and I am a better person from knowing the outstanding Howard and Tristan Rodman. She taught me that grace under pressure, intellectual rigor, and profound generosity are not mutually exclusive qualities. She was a singularity in the field, and I know that film studies, media studies, visual studies are far richer and better because of her. Radical thinkers who are also deeply selfless colleagues, mentors, and leaders are rare in this or any other field. Anne's scholarly work on theory, history, and visuality will continue to influence us and live on in her absence. I sadly bark out to her here, missing the person I, as an adult, have looked up to the most. Losing her has been unspeakably hard but knowing her made me better—as a person and a scholar.

In this era of multitasked work and leisure, the two bleed together more often than not. I have mined my own friendships for scholarly pursuits and my scholarly pursuits have yielded great friendships. This book began under the good guidance of such colleagues and friends. Peter Feng, Chris McNamara, Gaylyn Studlar, Bambi Haggins, Kristen Whissel, Catherine Benamou, Philip Hallman, Lucia Saks, Terri Sarris, Daniel Herbert, Mark Kligerman, Manishita Dass, Jim Pyke, Aswin Punathambekar, and Stashu Kybartas have all been sounding boards and astute critics of my work. Abé Markus Nornes, Richard Abel, and Johannes Von Moltke deserve special mention for their support and guidance. New media scholars and colleagues Eric Faden, Mark J. P. Wolf, Raiford Guins, and Heidi Cooley have been important in shaping my thoughts and making my writing better. Rhona Berens still reads my work even now, and my writing group just plain rocks. Students, staff, and friends Alex Ebel, Stephanie Wooten, and Carrie Moore have kept me on track despite all the glorious distractions television and new media routinely present. Erin Hanna deserves a special award for Most Assists on a Manuscript for her keen, insightful, and precise work on many aspects of this book, especially the index and bibliography. Jennifer Hardacker, Amy Parsons, Sally Johnson, and Kelly Beissel amaze and inspire me. And it would be remiss of me to not mention some of the monkey boys—Javier Grillo-Marxuach was generous with his precious time and transmedia ideas, and John Corey was a good sounding board. Indeed, they are damn dirty apes. And finally, family: Stephen Johnson is an ideal research subject and a wonderful partner too, while Christopher, Elisa, and Luke Murphy help anchor me in the real. Mary Louise Murphy, all ninety-six years and ninety-six pounds of her, has taught me how to have faith, to persevere, and to do it all with humility. David J. Murphy has always supported my academic efforts, even in such dubious and unstable fields as art history, visual studies, and media studies.

Written in an era of downsized university presses and budgets, this book was almost entirely supported by funding from various University of Michigan units: the Teaching with Technology Institute, the Center for Research, Learning and Teaching, and Instructional Support Services all aided and enabled my writing. Critically timed support from the College of Literature, Science, and Arts Deans' Office was also necessary and crucial to finishing this work. David Rodowick

and Jeffrey Sconce, along with my colleagues in Screen Arts
and Cultures at the University of Michigan, gave me excellent feedback at my departmental manuscript workshop, and
the anonymous readers at Rutgers University Press helped
me see my way through to the best realization of my ideas.
Leslie Mitchner at Rutgers has supported and believed in this
project from the beginning, and her impeccably professional staff
patiently and thoroughly made this manuscript into a book. I
am especially indebted to Katie Keeran and Margaret Case for
their tireless and adept efforts on the manuscript's pages. And
yet, it goes without saying that all flaws and flies in the ointment
here are entirely my own.

My students are the reason why I do what I do: I teach them,
they teach me, and together we work toward ideas like those
found here. Thank you, thank you, thank you: you know who
you are. Portions of this manuscript were originally presented at
the New Media Center at the University of California, Berkeley;
the University of California, Irvine; and the Society for Cinema
and Media Studies Chicago, Vancouver, Philadelphia, and almost
Tokyo. Very early, preliminary incarnations of chapters 1 and
4 appeared in the *Video Game Theory Reader 2.0* (New York:
Routledge, 2009) and the *Journal of Visual Culture* 4.1 (2004),
respectively.

And finally, I did save some surprise for those who made
it to the end of this section. Jasper, Mary, Allie, William, and
especially Winston Murphy-Johnson all witnessed, lived, and
endured the time it took to write this book more than anyone
else. For that, they, each an exemplar of their companion species,
deserve both treats and perhaps even a trip to the dog park or
a date with some catnip.

How Television
Invented New Media

INTRODUCTION

How Television Invents
New Media

Hi, I'm Conan O'Brien and I'm here to tell
you about an exciting new technology called
television! Television allows you to watch
things just as you would on your computer
or cell phone except while seated in a
more comfortable chair. Television, why not
watch some tonight?
—June 2009 promotion for *The Tonight Show*

I had a show. Then I had a different show.
Now I have a Twitter account.
—Conan O'Brien's Twitter bio, 2010

As a child I was fascinated by television—
not just the programming, which I was enthralled by, but the set
itself. The 1970s-era television set I knew as a girl had UHF and
VHF knobs for selecting channels, and smaller, stick-like, twist-
able controls to adjust tint, vertical hold, horizontal hold, and
other elements related to picture quality. A speaker was hidden
behind a plastic grill and the sides, though they were also plastic,
had faux wood-grain patterns on them. This set, a nineteen-inch
color model, sat on a cart with chrome legs and "wood" shelves.
It was what we now call, in retrospect, analog television (figure
1). Early on, the TV wore a "rabbit ears" antenna, which my
brothers and I continually adjusted so a program would "come

1. A mid-twentieth-century television and its owner, via Flickr.

in" from the broadcast spectrum with the best image and sound quality. Often, when dusting the set or in stolen moments alone with the TV, I'd play with those knobs—saturating the tint of the characters onscreen, turning and turning each knob to see how it functioned and how the image could be distorted.

In the early 1980s, television sets began to change. More and more cabinet-model televisions—hulking pieces of wood (or manufactured wood) furniture, became larger, with bigger screens. These sets were often accompanied by ancillary television technologies such as cable boxes and video cassette recorders. TV speakers could boast stereo sound, each speaker enrobed in fine mesh fabric behind a wood latticed cover held within the television cabinet itself.

I recently remembered my childhood encounters with television sets while staying in a newly built hotel. My room was divided into a public area with seating and a more private section with a bed. In between, on each side of a floor-to-ceiling central wood wall that ran through the middle of the space, were two flat screen, forty-two-inch television sets, which allowed guests to luxuriate and watch TV either in bed or on the couch. The screens filled nearly the entire width of the wall, which also conveniently contained all of their cables and wiring. Flat, matte-black, and only accessible with remote controls, these televisions hung on the wall like giant, empty framed paintings, waiting to be filled with content on demand. Unlike the knobs, plastic grills, speakers, and antennae of my childhood, these televisions did not entice one to reach out and physically touch them. Instead, all of those adjustments previously made by turning a knob or adjusting a rabbit-ear were now made through the remote control and its programmed, on-screen menu. As so often is the case when I watch television—both the television sets themselves and the programming—I was reminded how television *is* new media: a deeply digital, interactive device mediated by the manipulation of both hardware (the remote) and software (the onscreen guide to the TV's settings and the program guide for navigating content).

Yet, as a medium, television's role in both the arrival of new media and the ways in which it delivers new media content to us is often minimized or overlooked by those who emphasize comparisons between new media and other forms of representation, or those who simply see television situated, however problematically, on one side of an old media/new media divide.[1]

In this book, I contend that our understanding of new media can be deepened by reconsidering television's role in the emergence of digital cultures and technologies. Furthermore, in engaging with television *as* new media, certain questions about the blind side of television studies emerge: for instance, why are video games, encountered almost exclusively through television technology, not considered an integral part of television studies? Aren't games also programs that viewers/gamers encounter through the TV? Doesn't the sustained engagement and interactivity of gamers with their televisions expand notions of "interactive television"?

How Television Invented New Media demonstrates that the concept of "new media" stretches back to an earlier historical moment, while also offering a deeper and more specific history of convergence between media forms. Although culture might always churn out and emphasize the "new," particularly when the culture in question is media culture, I suggest that "new media" should actually be understood as an historical term that emerged with the rise of personal computing and computer networks and carries with it the baggage of a utopian, emancipatory set of beliefs about reconfiguration of the Self, the Social, and the Real through simulation and virtuality. By analyzing the new media polemic and reconnecting television to its proper place in new media history, we can more aptly and precisely see how television invented new media—and how new media continues to reinvent television.

In the past few decades, once seemingly discrete media technologies such as film, television, and computers have increasingly coalesced through the industrial convergence of production and delivery methods and the narrative crossovers and linkages now commonly found between co-positioned media objects such as film franchises, television programs, or the adaptation of one medium's content into another format. There are also media products whose production is underwritten by corporate conglomerates with financial interests spread across multiple markets that can be synergistically utilized to support the larger conglomerate's interests. Today this is seen when a television network's advertising time, or increasingly, time within a network program's narrative, is mobilized to support the theatrical release of a film produced by another division of the larger corporation.[2]

Such shifts in the established methods of media production have emerged alongside new forms such as mobile episodes or online series, Web sites, fan-authored content, blogs, Twitterfeeds, alternate reality games (ARGs), viral marketing strategies, and mobile software applications ("apps"). In addition to these changes, there have also been tremendous changes in how, when, and where one accesses, uses, views, reads, plays, or hears media today, as digital technologies with multitasking capabilities often allow for media consumption across a seemingly ever-increasing range of devices and in a variety of shifting locales. In 2010, one can easily watch *Strangers on a Train* (Hitchcock, 1951) on a train or play the air combat game *Tom Clancy's H.A.W.X.* (2009) on one's iPhone while on an airplane, as long as the phone is in "airplane" mode. With the rise of digital technologies as part of the production, distribution, and consumption of media culture, the media landscape has thus changed dramatically—and continues to do so at a fast pace. This is not a book solely about those changes, though these shifting conditions are relevant to what this book is about, which is how television—as a technology, as a cultural institution, and as a part of everyday life—has been and continues to be a key paradigm for understanding and using contemporary digital media culture and its operations.

What Is Television?

In order to argue successfully for television's place in new media's history, present and future, it is important to first be clear about what I mean when I say "television," especially because television as a term and as a part of media cultures around the world means many different things. Television is, in fact, more a set of connected ideas, beliefs, and technologies than it is any one thing that can be reduced to the home electronics device with a screen that might be found in a living room, bedroom, kitchen, bathroom, or other space within a home or in a doctor's office, airport, bar, or electronics store.

"Television" is a word whose meaning has been expanded and applied to so many different things that using the term precisely can be difficult—the word has become an abstraction. Certainly it is the case that "television" is often invoked in broad strokes that gesture toward a vast range of media content, distribution practices, industries, viewers, and viewing practices. In common parlance, "television" can refer to a television receiver or set, or a particular program, or the entire field and history of media made for and broadcast or relayed and delivered via television technologies, or particular television networks, production companies, or distribution companies. How then does one talk about television as a term profoundly in flux whose meaning shifts depending upon a particular context?

The way in which I have approached television here is to think of television as a figure (or perhaps more like a kind of fugue state?) in the cultural imagination. Although the meanings associated with television continue to circulate and change, understanding television as part of the contemporary cultural imagination also allows us to see TV not just through televisual representations, nor just through its industries (which include everything from satellite and cable to advertising to set repair), nor just as a medium of representation that sometimes goes by the name "video," nor just as a set of historical objects, texts, and technologies. Industry scholar Amanda Lotz offers a productive model for imagining television through the following modes: "Television as an electronic public sphere; Television as a subcultural form; Television as a window on other worlds; and Television as a self-determined gated community" (42). Lotz's televisual modes help to clarify the ever-shifting rhetoric surrounding the medium. Although I have not adopted all of Lotz's categories here, I share her interest in how the medium of television can simultaneously take on and occupy such a wide range of rhetorical positions as both new medium and old, window on the world and public sphere, or as communities of viewers utilizing specific technologies.

By conjuring forth television from the cultural imagination (which, of course, is really the imaginations of many cultures), one can call to mind how television is all of these things at once, and yet still an abstract way of talking about "the vision of distant objects obtained . . . [via] a system for reproducing an actual or recorded scene at a distance on a screen," as the *Oxford English Dictionary* tells us.[3]

Why is this important? In declaring that television has invented new media, I am using this broader conception of television as a way around the tendency to think of television abstractly and as a way back into the moments where specific instances of television or the televisual have acted as precursor, precedent, or contingent element joined with new media (another abstract term). "Television" is a word that can conjure up many forms of TV representations and genres, the development of synergistic technologies, and the deployment of strategies to link television to computers—and then link computers and Internet content back into television. In fact, it is the very flexible and slippery rhetoric of television that makes it such a crucial tool for understanding new media. Television is *not* one set thing in this book: instead I intend for the term television to resonate across the range of devices, situations, businesses, and uses that TV does in fact cross into, occupy, mediate, and even "contaminate" in contemporary life.

Television is a daily fact of existence for many today—from its role as electronic roommate and white noise device to its imagined perspective in the films that comment upon the medium, like *Being There* (Ashby, 1979) or *The Truman Show* (Weir, 1998).[4] Television has become an architectural component; television is part of spaces both private and public—from living rooms to hair salons, restaurants, airports, and bars (McCarthy, 9). Television operates as an abstraction, as imagined in everything from the logic of the once ubiquitous "Kill Your Television" bumper sticker and the deeply ingrained beliefs about the medium as a whole that the bumper sticker espouses, to the way in which we commonly measure taste according to particular mediums or genres. For instance, one might watch television but only watch pay cable series, such as those produced by Home Box Office, a network known for its slogan "It's not TV, it's HBO." This genius bit of marketing simultaneously presents HBO product as something qualitatively different from "TV"—something that, it implies, is worth watching and paying for. Both "TV" and "HBO" in this account gesture toward grand notions of product and experience quality (or lack thereof) and rely upon our received idea of just what "TV" is. Television is a conduit for both informational discourses and a wide array of narrative and representational genres of entertainment media. As a range of devices and ancillary technological components (VCRs, DVD players, digital video recorders, video game systems, to name some of the most common), "television" is deeply familiar and still retains some sheen of technological "magic" as a complex technology that users primarily interact with through its screen interface and remote controls.

Just as journalist Tom Standage argued that the nineteenth-century development of the telegraph and telegraph networks prefigures the communications systems of the Internet in his book *The Victorian Internet: The Remarkable Story of the Telegraph and the Nineteenth-Century's On-Line Pioneers* (1998), the various incarnations of television as technology, industry, media culture, and visual discourse are, in fact, an analog precursor of the World Wide Web, which prefigures such technologies as personal computers, computer networks, mobile communications devices, and all those elements we have come to know and understand as digital media. What is more, television's role in the emergence of "new" media is far from over: television continues to be part of the process and emergence of the new, as televisual content migrates to new devices and screens and new devices are developed to maximize and expand our very notion of the televisual itself.

Perhaps one of the most productive approaches to television that a reader of this book could embrace is to think of television as a "middletext," a concept that I will discuss at greater length in chapter 2. In its very pervasiveness and abstraction of form, as well as its ability to contain and present other media, television is well positioned in the (historical, aesthetic, and technological) middle of our media system today. Although I have no interest in subjugating one media to another or in reconstructing dated hierarchies that place television as a lesser or "other" medium to film, I think it is time to recuperate the "middleness" of television as a productive quality. Indeed, William Uricchio has pointed out how "film's own history and developmental trajectory, and its assumed agency with regard to 'derivative' media such as television, have been recast in the light of an array of precedent technologies, practices, and notions of mediation" ("Historicizing" 23).

With its longer history, larger screen, and more established lineage connecting cinema to theater and literature, the film medium has long occupied a more "artistic" reputation than television. Yet this new era of digital technologies and media convergence presents an opportunity for rethinking television outside of its traditional, received notion as a domestic consumer technology or "idiot box." Television scholar William Boddy, whose own work traces the marketing discourses and reception of television technologies, puts it this way: "The current period of confusion and conflict among the would-be architects of our putative post-television age offers a productive site to investigate the ways in which wider social, technological, and political changes may deform or put into crisis such calculated representations of media apparatus and artifact" ("Redefining the Home Screen," 191). Boddy's language here—that these changes may "deform" or cause a "crisis" for media technologies and artifacts—is quite telling about how high the stakes are for how films (as well as for TV, computers, and networks) are configured as experiences and objects for users to encounter, consume, and engage with. Indeed, the very abstractness of television and the flexible, fluid formlessness of the digital seemingly encourage a slipperiness around their use, aesthetics, and presence in our lives. Yet such abstraction can, in fact, be productive for approaching both the distinct qualities associated with a medium and for understanding how—at what point and in what uses—media comes together and converges.

Within the fields of film and media studies, there has been a division among approaches to "media" in this contemporary era that is marked by the convergence of previously distinct forms. Sometimes it is increasingly difficult to separate or define where one medium stops and another starts. On the one hand are those who prioritize medium specificity, who attempt to distill the unique properties that are essential to distinct media, be it film, television, or literary texts. This attention to medium specificity is often linked with the methodologies of media archaeology, which will be discussed at greater length in chapter 3. Other scholars have approached media in a seemingly opposite way, stressing how once separate forms of media now converge, often as a result of digital processes. As David Thorburn and Henry Jenkins put it in *Rethinking Media Change: The Aesthetics of Transition*, "Medium-specific approaches risk simplifying technological change to a zero-sum game in which one medium gains at the expense of its rivals. A less reductive, comparative approach would recognize the complex synergies that always prevail among medium systems, particularly during periods shaped by the birth of a new medium of expression" (3). Like Jenkins and Thorburn's comparative approach, thinking of television as a middletext that is between other media proves useful here, as does addressing television as a technology that "glues" together the old and new in terms of style, industry, and technology.

WHY "NEW MEDIA"?

The study of digital technologies such as computers, software, video games, and virtual reality systems has, in the course of establishing itself, entailed its own production of new words and terms—its own discursive formations, as Michel Foucault would say. Early works in the field often used the prefix *cyber-*, drawing upon 1990s claims about cyberculture and cyberspace, both terms describing the newly virtual realms and activities made possible by advances in computing technology and inspired by science fiction literature. Scholars today often label work on similar subjects as "new media" or "digital media" studies. New media work tends to use the prefix "new" to signal the philosophical and epistemological roots of the field, since it indicates an aspect of the media being examined as permanently in flux, always producing its own rhetoric of the just-in-time, definitely not-old. Meanwhile, digital media is the study of just that: media produced in, by, on, or accessed through digital means (that is, through the computer or encoded and using binary digits). To use one term or the other is to take a side in the debate about how technology itself is meaningful in media culture today—is it through its newness or through reference to its specific technological and computerized parts? I have attempted to be consistent in my use of these two terms but must admit some slippage—I believe that sometimes the specific technologies are indeed more important than the larger rhetoric of new media. Also, when referencing other scholars I use the terms that they themselves take up in their work, which might reflect the moment or locations from which that author approaches this new field.

An early goal of this project was to reassert the visuality of new media: to think just as rigorously about its images as its words and its modes of textuality. That goal remains a part of this current version of the project, but one must always be careful with words, even if we simply want to use them to talk about images. A good friend of mine has set her computer background image to display a graphic of a computer monitor that also displays a sky filled with fluffy clouds, emblazoned with text that reads, *Ceci n'est pas une ordinateur* (This is not a computer).[5] Indeed, we must realize a picture of a computer is not a computer; it is first and foremost a representation, and we use words to access those. I want to assure you, the reader, that every effort has been made to make the words used here clear, precise, and specific, even if the context in which they are used or the objects they reference are always fluctuating, changeable, flowing, free-form, and unfixed in time and/or space. It would be much easier to study new media were it fixed in amber or under glass, but we will have to make do with how it does appear instead.

What Is This New in New Media?

New media refers to emergent digital media forms—those generated with computers as the primary instrumentation responsible for the structure and appearance of certain objects—as well to media forms and technologies that have been reprocessed, in some cases even digitized, by computers. This new media generated by computer can be anything from a scene in a film that is reliant on the insert of digital objects into a frame (the background, a central character, or even a particular item) to a flash animation on a Web site, initiated by the entry of a site address into a Web browser that then contacts the server or host machine for the site and reveals a pre-programmed element—a flying object or perhaps music—that the user confronts as part of the site. Video and computer games, as pieces of software operated by users (gamers), are also found within this category of new media.

New media can also refer to media forms and technologies that have been reprocessed and are often found where computers present an alternative, assumed to be technologically superior, option for a previously existing type of medium. In some cases, these new media adaptations wholly replace analog or traditional processes, while in others the digital element is an additive part of a process. To further complicate this, these cases of digital remediation might attempt to mimic the technology that is being usurped, as in digital cameras that utilize a shutter "click" sound effect when capturing a photo; or the new media process might appear and be experienced quite differently, as in the way that digital video recorders fast forward through digital frames of a program rather than skip forward through an image recorded onto tape by a traditional video recorder.

It is easier, and far, far more slippery, to simply call a digital media process, technology, software program, object, or installation by the name "new media" (or digital media), than to specify what and how it is that a particular medium (again, the best examples here are television programs, Internet Web sites, and video games) might qualify or be presented as new. It is much more likely that such a "new media" is partially new in its representations, technologies, or delivery methods but still has some "old media" vestigial remnants remaining. No one, however, from individual scholars to the university presidents and provosts who set technology agendas, wants to proclaim themselves or their institution a center for semi-new, emerging, rhetoric-laden technologies, media, and the cultures that make and use them.

The problem about studying the present—or even the recent past—is that it is never over, and one is very much entangled and enmeshed within the discourse of the day. Critical distance, that much-lauded academic quality that allows one to understand the social, economic, historically inflected context of a cultural production, is elusive when that medium and its attendant technologies are right there in front of us, part of our regularly self-scheduled programs and processes. As Bruce Sterling evocatively put it in the introduction to the short story collection *Mirrorshades: The Cyberpunk Anthology* (1986), authors writing in the mode of cyberpunk science fiction recognized how "technology is visceral . . . it is pervasive, utterly intimate.

Not outside us, but next to us. Under our skin; often, inside our minds. Technology itself has changed. Eighties tech sticks to the skin, responds to the touch: the personal computer, the Sony Walkman, the portable telephone, the soft contact lens" (xi).[6]

While Sterling's list of 1986s seemingly futuristic technologies might seem quaint to us today in 2010, his description of how the then-new media was new tells us something about what is considered new—that which is personal, responsive, mobile, attached or near the body, pervasive. With the Sony Walkman, the PC, and the portable phone, we actually see the predecessors to some of our contemporary moment's most hyped and "innovative" technologies: the digital media player, the mobile phone, and networked computer technology.[7] For many today, the line between one's self and one's new media is convincingly blurred—making the abstractions of the new all the more powerful and crucial to understand. In the 2000s, individuals make, mark, and remake both the media that they consume and themselves via these media. How can one have critical distance and a deeper understanding of devices that one gives nicknames to, amends with digital photographs of loved ones, places inside customized holders, or plasters over with stickers? And while it can be quite difficult to separate ourselves from pervasive, routine, mobile, personal, and responsive digital media technologies, it is crucial to understand and interrogate both their operations on us and our operations of them. To do this it makes sense, then, to begin with television, the electronic media technology that prefigures our current state of moving-image and media saturation.[8]

LEAVING REALITY BEHIND:
LIFE INSIDE SCREENS

Television was first widely launched in the United States as part of a postwar economic boom and reorganization of culture around the emerging suburban communities, newly built homes, and newly available consumer and household goods. Television was but one new technology for living, and one that gathered together families and neighbors around the screen.[9] Other new technologies of the early 1950s were modern but not screen-based; new appliances for household chores included washing machines, dryers, refrigerators, and modern stoves with built-in ovens. Many had "windows" that allowed one to watch the new modern processes that made the home hygienic and up-to-date (Spigel, *Make Room for TV* 127–135). In 2010, on the other hand, middle-American homes and contemporary life are inundated with screens and communications devices: digital control touch screens for heat and air conditioning, digital microwave control panels, television sets, computer screens, mobile phones, global positioning systems with touch screens, networked media servers, video game consoles, mobile music players with touch screens. This multiplication of screens and the concomitant increased mediation and interaction are part of everyday American experience today, just as the stainless steel-framed windows and softly curving geometry of washers, dryers, and refrigerators were part of the postwar experience. But what does it mean that we are so comfortable with performing daily tasks and functions via screens? Is it really possible to trace these screens back to television's initial domestic presence? What is lost when we turn to or embed ourselves in the processes we encounter on screens? I began to think about this in earnest when the economic conditions of actual life crept into my scholarly project a few years ago, as the collapse of the local economy led me to rethink how much time, identification, and engagement with screens was possible once productive employment in the actual, physical environment became scarce.

FROM CATCHALL TO ESCAPE HATCH

A few years ago I purchased a copy of the computer game *World of Warcraft* (2004), with the intent to study it and potentially use it in a course I teach on video games and culture. My partner, a software architect, quickly usurped ownership and began to spend more and more time each day in Azeroth, the imaginary "world" in which the game's warcraft takes place. Many things about what quickly became a digital gaming obsession for him were fascinating and disturbing for me, as a media scholar, to observe. Not only did I find myself perusing "WoW Widow" Web sites that offered support for those whose loved ones had succumbed to life in the game over life in the Real, but also I was also amazed to witness the slippage between my partner and his virtual selves. His game avatars, both his primary character he played the game as and his secondary, more experimental characters, quickly obtained social status via virtual accomplishments, found and earned customized weapons and armor, and joined in a tight-knight virtual community of likeminded individuals. The people behind these avatars were of a wide range of ages and backgrounds—retired couples played together, parents played the game with their children, people of many different ethnic and cultural backgrounds were united . . . in their desire to play in the virtual space of the game.

And although there are perhaps skill-based, strategic accomplishments in the game and it has a deeply involved hierarchical ranking system, the game spaces of *World of Warcraft* are also deeply stereotypical of fantasy role-playing games and the fantasy genre in general. There are castles and keeps, city squares, giant mythological monsters, idyllic meadows, and dangerous passes in Azeroth. It also has a range of systems based on real-world counterparts—for instance, an eBay-like auction component is a key part of the game, and a good deal of time is spent dealing with questions of transportation (should one take the zeppelin, the hippogriff, or the gryphon taxi?). Yet what it does not have is just as compelling: in Azeroth there is no crumbling IT (information technology) economy, as existed in Michigan when my partner began playing the game most avidly. Underemployed and with few opportunities to pursue, he elected to exist in a world where he could be a productive member of its society. While there is strife in this virtual world, along with warring factions and an untold number of monsters to slay, problems like poverty, low social status, or a lack of education (as reflected by a low game rank) are fairly easily overcome via determination, exploration, and just plain time spent playing the game and solving its problems, unlike the situation in nonvirtual lived experiences. In *World of Warcraft*, one's character's problems can eventually be solved through effort, whereas outside *this virtual world* things often get and stay far messier, and the hard worker does not always get the reward. *World of Warcraft* is a meritocracy; life is not.

These virtual interactions, which can allow one to moderate reality and intersperse it with virtual cultures, accomplishments, and status, can act as a kind of balm for the Real—a way to soften its harsh edges. This aspect of new media—its alternate social worlds and "realities"—was much remarked upon during the first wave of new media scholarship, which typically celebrated the virtual while critiquing naïve attempts to escape the Real. This scholarship echoes earlier critiques of other media forms—both film and television—and their escapist tendencies. Interestingly, my partner's approach to *World of Warcraft* also speaks to the multiple screens and digital devices that one uses regularly—all those digital screens, mobile devices, and meditating tools now routinely available. Using two computer monitors, he plays the game on one and keeps the other for e-mail, coding, and to use as a movie and TV screen, listening to the audio through headphones.[10] From time to time he switches headphones to use "teamspeak," an ancillary software program that groups of players use to communicate with and collaborate with each other in-game.

I tell this tale of my own encounter with *World of Warcraft* not to condemn the game or its cultures and economies, which are truly amazing in their depth and complexity.[11] Instead I think the best way to understand the phenomenon is to look more closely at new media forms themselves, at where they come from and what they promise to do, and to consider how digital technologies are often understood, simultaneously, as both an escape hatch from the Real and a catchall for a wide range of objects and experiences. In approaching the new through both these terms, one can, it is hoped, do an end run around the overblown rhetoric so often attached to new media and confront the varied cultures and representations that the term routinely refers to. Perhaps, given our state's abysmal economy at the time, gaining confidence and building team skills inside a game was actually a productive use of my partner's unexpected time off from "real work." We need to ask why these frameworks of escapism, fantasy, endless possibility, and alternate realities are so often applied to new media as new forms emerge, whether the "new media" in question is a cathode ray tube television receiver or a thin, touch screen networked tablet computer.

THE INVENTION OF NEW MEDIA

I was working out the shape and scope of the original skeleton of this book for quite some time before I fully realized what its core claims about new media and television were. I believe this is because the new media experiences, theorizations, and intellectual trajectories I take on here are entangled with objects and experiences that we are repeatedly told are *not* about thought, culture, production, or worth. Rather, new media such as the Internet, and its cultures, computer networks, video games, and television programs, are often unpredictably part of day-to-day life in meaningful ways. As Marshall McLuhan put it, "We shape our tools and thereafter our tools shape us."

Yet theories of new media and, in fact, the whole field of new media/digital culture studies have historically manifested in ways that create a blind spot overshadowing these quotidian media cultures. To discuss how this happened, we must trace out how new media studies has emerged, in what venues and through what voices. New media studies, also known as cyberculture studies or digital media studies, is a very young field that is still developing its methodologies and its disciplinary boundaries. The time is ripe for an intervention into the practice of new media scholarship, such as the argument here.[12] In fact, even though the title of this book perhaps seems self-evident when uttered aloud, and yet, for many years, television's role in the history of new media was often elided in favor of comparisons between even older media forms (like cinema and text) and what was emerging as new (computers). In order to understand how television invented new media, it is worth explaining why television's role in new media history and culture is often minimized and overlooked.

All too often the formative texts and theories in the emerging field of new media studies have, perhaps unwittingly, created both a hierarchy of media types and a set of connections and comparisons that link new media to cinema while often overlooking television's contributions to how new media is approached and understood. For instance, Lev Manovich's influential *The Language of New Media* (2001) insists upon a complicated set of connections between computers and cinema that include literal links between cinematic and computational "software" (film stock as a medium upon which computer programs could be imprinted) and the "languages" of representation that both computer code and films "speak" (330–331), as discussed below. In contrast to this extended comparison with cinema, Manovich's book only mentions television briefly and in passing. This minimizing of television's influence on new media is typical of how film and media scholars have approached the digital age. Film theorist Vivian Sobchack's early comparative essay "The Scene of the Screen: Envisioning Photographic, Cinematic, and Electronic 'Presence,'" first published in *Materialities of Communication* in 1994, goes to some length to conflate the digital and televisual as "electronic," and yet the "electronic" is presented as a less engaging, more diffuse experience than the cinematic. A later version of the essay, published in Sobchack's *Carnal Thoughts: Embodiment and Moving Image Culture* (2004), actually expands upon her initial grouping of the digital and televisual while retaining her original critique: "Digital electronic technology atomizes and abstractly schematizes the analogic quality of the photographic and cinematic into discrete pixels and bits of information that are then transmitted serially, each bit discontinuous, and absolute—each bit 'being in itself' even as it is part of a system" (153). Although Sobchack does not specify what she means by "digital electronic" here, her next sentence goes on to list how, in her mind, television and the digital have already converged as: "television, videocassettes, and digital discs, VCR and DVD recorder/players, electronic games, personal computers with Internet access, and pocket electronics of all kinds" (153). And yet these "digital electronic" devices do not have quite the same impact as cinema and its spatio-temporal "presence." Instead, the "digital electronic" "atomizes" those very elements right out of photography and cinema, respectively.

For scholars approaching digital media from within the

disciplines of film studies or film and media studies, certain historical precursors and analogies have appeared as seemingly intuitive, automatic frames of reference for understanding what marks new media as new and what still grounds it in broader historical and theoretical fields. The early years of cinema have been mined as crucial analogies for understanding the early years of digital media and its uncertainties of format, exhibition, and aesthetic. The media scholars Jay David Bolter and Richard Grusin compare the present conditions of digital media to Tom Gunning's much-cited "cinema of attractions" model in their key text *Remediation: Understanding New Media* (155–158, 254).[13] Although it is surely the case that the early days of cinema and its period of development are instructional for understanding the current state and development of digital media technologies, this overemphasis upon the parallels between certain examples of so-called "old media" (namely cinema) and New Media (such as computers, digital devices, computer networks, and a range of other technologies, not all of which are image-based) leaves out a crucial historical predecessor of new media: television.

Even scholars who do contend with televisual forms in their work on new media often find cinema's dominance in the field as something to contend with and to incorporated into their study.[14] For other scholars, the jury is still out on just what forms the "formlessness" of new media will encompass. In 2002, Dan Harries's editorial sections of *The New Media Book* tell us:

> It would be difficult to deny that there have been significant shifts in the cinema and television industries toward increased digitization at the levels of production, post-production, distribution and exhibition.... Such shifts pose many new and old questions regarding the status of media identity. Can new media find its own voice, its own vision—detached from the traditions of the cinematic and the televisual? Can we draw a meaningful differentiation between new technologies and their older media siblings? And what can we learn about film and television through the exploration of digital media? (207)

Clearly Harries's questions are still relevant to understanding both new and old media today. *The New Media Book* goes to great pains to consider television alongside cinema, dedicating an entire section of the volume to old media/new media comparisons that intermingle cinema, television, and new media. This comparative media approach came after a scholarly publishing frenzy that lasted for several years and was typified by fashionable anthologies thematically organized around cyber-modalities and identities.[15] A new scholarly field centered on emerging technologies and industries that were receiving a great deal of attention legislatively, economically, and culturally around the globe, "new media" was a hot topic in the 1990s. As such, attempts to anchor all this newness to modes of experience that were widely understood and studied made sense. Literature scholars developed studies of hypertext and began to examine hypertext as genre and structure for writing.[16] In this context, film scholars' comparisons between emerging digital forms and cinema follows a valid logic, as well as reflecting the anxieties that new media visualities raise for historical forms of cinema and of celluloid, both of which came under economic and material scrutiny. Digital technology was widely believed at the time to be cheaper to produce and distribute, beliefs that industry scholar John Caldwell has largely debunked in his work.[17]

As the field of new media studies has emerged and grown, it has become increasingly specialized. Niche subfields like video game studies, digital textualities, virtual community analysis, visual and digital effects studies, and software studies exist in dialogue with more established disciplines such as anthropology, cinema studies, communication studies, and media theory. The wide range of journals, both traditional and online, that have developed since 1993 attest to the intellectual and public fascination with how new technologies and new media have come to matter.[18] Although there is undoubtedly great value in such niche approaches, *How Television Invented New Media* comes at the cultural "problem" or phenomena of new media and digital cultures through an understanding of the complex inter-relatedness of the digital, that is, texts and objects written in and understood through the "language of new media." Using a methodological approach informed by visual studies, *How Television Invented New Media* puts the analytical, textual, and cultural logics of video games, television, software, hardware, networks, and computing culture into contact with one another in order to trace out and, indeed, to uncover how new media became "new" and how we, its users, use it.[19] Prior to the discourse of new media, of course, there were innovative technologies, including those that utilized computer elements. Mainframe, micro- and personal computers, and their predecessors existed and were imagined (by scientists and mathematicians like Ada Lovelace, Charles Babbage, and Alan Turing, not to mention science fiction novelists like Philip K. Dick and William Gibson, who imagined computers as part of the future long before such imagined technologies were viable) before terms like "new media" came into use. The way we imagine and talk about technologies, how we frame them as "new" or "old" or "futuristic" is critical and even predictive about how they will come to be understood. The accelerated rate of advancement in computer technology and production allows us to be already in possession of "old" new media, even when we open the box to peek inside for the first time.

This book is a serious investigation of stuff that people do with computer technologies and media such as television. This is stuff that is not always serious or even particularly scholarly (how does one explain the fame cycle of Dramatic Chipmunk [prairie dog] or the other Internet memes that appear in the 2008 Weezer video "Pork and Beans"?).[20] New media must be taken seriously. But "taking it seriously" need not involve taking the fun out of the enterprise. New media is and can be fun. To turn the cult Playstation 2 game *Katamari Damacy* (2004), with its revelatory, high-energy, joyful explorations of space, volume, and scale into a dry academic text where one solely analyzes, say, its rhetoric of consumption, is to render its own logic dead and void through the act of analysis. These are not like old and new, television and digital, as oppositional perspectives but about how two parts form a greater whole. This is how and why "play matters" in uncovering how television invented new media.[21]

Academics, especially in the humanities, vigorously, routinely, and with great focus play with concepts and ideas, tackling rhetoric and untangling woeful maladies of logic. And yet such play is often divorced from and understood separately from the embodied, joyous acts one takes on in traditional modes of play, as has been argued by scholars Vivian Sobchack and Janet Murray, who each presents the deep ways that bodies produce knowledge in their works on embodiment, subjectivity, and agency.[22] In order to best understand new media, we must understand how new media forms engage their own logics of play. How does my iPhone make typing text messages a game of word identification and "keyboard" character manipulation? How do I play in GoogleMaps, retracing the paths between each of the places I've lived, via map view and street view? How do I try to "trick" or "beat" the television schedule through my programming of my DVR? All of these everyday acts are acts of play. Digital tools and toys invite us to play, experience, live in their forms. The moments when we click on the quick-play flash game or replay the unwinnable game *Space Invaders* (1978) for the five millionth futile time, when we step on the brand name in the multiplex advertising installation or follow a link and become embedded in the discourse of an alternate reality game urging us, however oddly, to "love bees" while learning a prehistory of the video/computer game *Halo* (2002), these moments embed us in a culture that hails us with an interactive address, an interpolation into play as a modality of life.[23] Play is all around us in this new millennium; we must understand how it works and how it works on us in order to see the ways in which both passive and active technologies are linked together in the new media moment.

THE DIGITAL DIURNAL; OR, WHERE DID ALL THE NEON GREEN GO?

In the earliest heyday of the field that has variously been called cyberculture, digital culture, and new media, scholars focused on technologies that offered virtual realities, immersive environments, and alternative social universes.[24] Coated in the neon colors of cyberpunk, theories, fictions, and representations emerged that imagined new media as escapist fantasias. In the intervening years, new media have become commonplace and are rarely evoked as the bright pulsing green networks of cyberspace anymore. New media is no longer so new, and it has lost some of its utopian sheen. What it has gained, though, is more solid footing in the diffusion of technologies and the rapid increase of media literacies. Today one no longer hopes to strap on goggles and gloves and enter some virtual brave new world. Instead we are content to encapsulate ourselves in iPod bubbles, each controlling our own media flows and traversing real and virtual spaces simultaneously. The digital is now the everyday: I wake to my digital alarm clock with its mp3 music feed, stumble out to the computer, check my e-mail, log on to social networking sites, turn on the radio or television, and go about my day. At each moment I am faced with the choices of mediated encounters: do I listen to the birds sing on my walk or talk on my phone instead? While I wait for an appointment do I login and play a game on the same phone-device? Dare I lecture without media tools? Is my car compliant and equipped with GPS, dual-purpose plug-in charger/adapters, Bluetooth? What will I make for dinner? Does my favorite food blog have that recipe I like? Where are my friends and colleagues and what are they up to, *right now*?[25] Increasingly, digital technologies offer convenient and often cheap answers to the problems of modern life—echoing the nondigital technologies that preceded them. Our daily rhythms, our diurnal routines, incorporate these machines, just as they incorporate us. As McLuhan put it, "The message of any medium or technology is the change of scale or pace or pattern that it introduces into human affairs" (*Understanding Media* 49). In chapter 3, I discuss how the television programming schedule both mirrors and creates a daily rhythm and structure for experience.[26]

As technologies such as television, computers, networks, and cell phones become habitual parts of twenty-first-century living—shaping the "scale or pace or pattern" of experience—questions about how those technologies and their content converge, overlap, and map onto one another become increasingly important to understanding how our lives are linked, bookmarked, guided, and put into the playlists of the technologies we use to mediate our surroundings.[27] At the same time that I am keenly aware of the everyday ways one encounters and plays with that which is labeled new, I am also deeply skeptical of the discourse of media convergence that has grown up around computers and media over the past decade.

Rethinking Convergence

Media convergence, as argued by Jenkins and others, is not in fact a result of new media but has existed for quite some time. And what does this convergence have to do with television? As Conan O'Brien's wry commentary in his 2009 *Tonight Show* promotion indicates, television's role in society is so culturally ingrained in our imaginations that we don't think of it (and we certainly don't imagine it as an "exciting new technology"), while we pay great attention to the high-tech machinations of computers, cell phones, and their networks. Yet television, watched from the comfort of our dens and family rooms, is a reliable, dependable technology and information/entertainment medium that predates and prefigures other innovations that deliver information and entertainment to our screens and fingertips. Of course it makes sense to think about how television invented new media. And yet . . . it takes some untangling of history, forms, ideologies, and media philosophies in order to understand just how television fits into the new media picture (see figure 2).

In its very ubiquity, television is also easy to forget or overlook. Its networks and my Internet network connection simultaneously soothe me—here are faraway places, friends, shops, and shows. When I go online I think of my "hacker" friends—computer network specialists who use one monitor or projection device for a wide range of audio and visual media— movies, games, music, e-mail—and who rarely acquire television through networks or legal channels.

Television, however, became key to this project—almost like a missing link—for talking about new media's visualities and experiences. It did not hurt that, at least theoretically, television's

2. Widescreen television set and Atari 400 computer: not technologically compatible without special adapters. *Is this convergence?*
(Photograph by the author.)

connections to new media have been minimized or overlooked
by scholars charting out the slippery and often seemingly imma-
terial terrain of new media studies, as discussed above. This
discourse can even been seen in the discourse surrounding new
media/old media productions like the television version of the
Web site *Funny or Die*. As reporter Jake Coyle put it, the television program

> *Funny or Die Presents* represents an increasingly common
> fusion between Web-created content and television. When
> the series was announced, [Will] Ferrell sarcastically asserted
> the deal was "the missing link moment where TV and
> Internet finally merge." The show is introduced by a 1950s-
> style TV host who intones: "*Funny or Die* is at the forefront
> of computer technology, leading the way in computer
> comedy programming. Tonight marks a departure from our

usual business model as we join the ever-declining world of broadcast television."[28]

The juxtaposition in *Funny or Die Presents* of the newness associated with "computer comedy programming" and the recognizable generic stereotype of the "1950s-style TV host" ironically announces the difference between old and new formats, just as the program is jokingly referred to as the "missing link" between television and the Internet.

When academics, in particular humanities scholars, first began to take note of the emerging cultures and forms that are today referred to as new media, they intuitively looked to other cultural phenomenon and leisure activities for comparison. Scholars engaged in such comparisons often question where the new might break with or rupture from the old, while also considering formal qualities that signal both continuities and breaks from the past. This dynamic, pitting old versus new in a narrative of progress, loss, innovation, or competition, unnecessarily creates an oppositional logic between industries, objects, and experiences that actually draw upon each other productively through moments of collaboration and reinvention as much as they "fight" each other off, as Caldwell has so aptly argued in his scholarship about media industries.[29]

TELEVISION INVENTED NEW MEDIA

Literally and figuratively, television informs how new media is used. This is a crucial role—television acts as a bridge between more historically established historical media forms and the emergent forms of new media as well as a theoretical model for computer use, spectatorship, and interactivity.

Literally and figuratively, television is the *ur-new medium*: in its postwar ubiquity, its connections via cable and satellite to larger information networks, its global reach, and its new technological and cultural forms. Televisual modes of reception have opened the door for consumer technologies and electronics such as personal computers, media players, and wireless phones. It is *the* medium that really is the message, as least when it comes to understanding the proliferation of screens, audiovisual technologies, and networks that are core parts of new media today.

From a strictly technological standpoint, television is closer to the computerized components of digital media culture than cinema is. Television receiver screen size and orientation and computer monitor size and orientation are similar to one another, largely because they rely upon similar technologies— first the cathode ray tube and later the liquid crystal display. Although this is not widely commented upon, many early personal computing technologies were first manufactured to connect to existing televisual technologies, turning the television receiver itself into a computer monitor. In fact, as chapter 1 ("This Is Intelligent Television") argues, the television receiver/ computer monitor hybridity of the 1970s helped to introduce and familiarize emerging personal computer and video game technologies. These early home computers—sometimes marketed as home video game systems and sometimes presented as educational toys or productivity tools—explicitly connected the routine domestic uses of television to the new experiences of computer interactivity, entertainment, and education.

In understanding the relationship between digital media and film and television, we can also note the way that projected cinematic images differ from the scanned images seen via a cathode ray tube or on a contemporary computer or televisual display. By situating the personal computer as a device accessible through the TV screen, this strategy of TV-as-monitor, born out of enthusiasts' practical and financial ingenuity to retrofit old technology to new, significantly situates computers within popular culture as a device both literally and symbolically connected to television. The TV-as-monitor strategy allowed manufacturers and users of early personal computer systems to (inadvertently) naturalize the computer as domestic technology with links (both literal and metaphorical) to television. Chapter 1 details how companies like Atari, Commodore, and Magnavox maximized the connections between televisions and computers that were made in the 1970s and early 1980s, during the first wave of popularity for home video game systems and personal computers. Devices that connect television and computers continue to proliferate, as chapter 3 will discuss, as part of the domestic discourse of personal computing and the discourse of media convergence and high-tech entertainment.

Today convergence is complicated by—and experienced more immediately through—the remapping of the globe by information networks. As French theorist Paul Virilio argues, we are now in an era dominated by speed and information, where there are no more journeys, only the instantaneous "arrival" of the computer user at a remote, virtual location (Virilio and Rose, *Open Sky* 16). It is possible for us to (virtually) converge ever further—using linguistic software to cross language barriers and low-cost routers to reroute information.[30]

AN INTERLUDE: NETWORKING TIME, SPACE, DISTANCE

I am in a small ship located somewhere close to the equator, surrounded by a group of Ecuadorian, Irish, Scottish, New Zealander, and Canadian people. As the boat rocks its way toward the port city of Puerta Ayora, Galapagos, Ecuador, we all gather around the television monitor and DVD player, watching a DVD compilation of short clips gathered from a wide range of Web sites and sources. Humiliating game shows lead into spectacular motorbike crashes, obese women in bikinis bounce atop unsuspecting men, beer commercials from Germany, Great Britain, and the United States stream across the screen. Periodically a Web site address is displayed for surfing crash videos or extreme sports sites. Everyone, despite national, regional, linguistic, class, race, and age differences, seems to *get* what they are seeing on the screen. So is this global visual culture, at last? Are we one world, united by the allure of the lowest common denominator?

Or is this instead a telling story not about media taste but about media legibility? Is this media convergence across platforms and the spectatorial boundaries? Is this yet another instance of bookmarking the television set?[31] For all our academic and social efforts to produce media literacy, the Internet is training us in a literacy all its own: the visual trick, joke, or disaster cuts across language and class—moments of recognition—of self-identification with humiliation, abjection, and the aberrant—that plays out in a few seconds on our television or computer screens (as, of course, we must remember they once did during the era of early cinema and its short film gags and displays).

This is also a telling story about space, distance, and the reach of information networks. Cut together into a compilation of recognizable media types, the images on the screen lose the markers of national and regional context in which they were made and become purely visual and musical snippets. Likewise, as viewers, my shipmates, and the crew members cross over and engage with this media despite being from Great Britain, Ecuador, Canada, New Zealand, and the United States. When I had booked my trip I had naively imagined the Galapagos as a location outside of information culture, untouched by satellite communications, cellular telephones, and computers—a place that still bore a resemblance to Charles Darwin's great natural laboratory. And while parts of Galapagos National Park are quite undisturbed by ecotourists like me, one can access data and voice communications quite easily from there, like most places on the planet. Information networks have shrunk the globe and distilled cultures into a vast, planetary "media culture," as both Virilio and McLuhan predicted.

Time is also reconfigured in this scenario. When one is always reachable, "on demand" and "in real time," our notion of how time is mediated is deeply lived and felt. While "real time" and "computer time" refer to the time that it takes for computer processes to render and produce data (often online video data is "streamed" in "real time"), being "on demand" is a phrase that has shifting meanings: we watch video "on demand," accessing files when we need or want them but we also are often "on demand" or "on call" ourselves, available virtually or telephonically for others who need our expertise. Our abilities to shift time via digital video recorders or maximize it via multi-tasking on digital devices also complicate how duration itself is experienced. Today, global positioning systems explain time in terms of distance, often updating that measurement based on live traffic updates. Yet "time," "distance," and "networks" are terms that collapse and fold into one another in a complex origami:

urbanites measure time by the frequency of trains arriving on a specific route while suburbanites calculate time based on the number of freeway exits they must pass to reach a destination. Children know time as the length of a media program or television episode ("You will go to bed after one *Dora the Explorer*."). To experience unmediated, unmeasured time is a great luxury in this century.

The intersection of this time-distance experience with computer networks is actually quite profound and speaks to an earlier moment of software convergence that underlies the structure of most digital media today. When smaller, local computer networks were first built, there was no mechanism in place that allowed for communication across and between networks. Without the ability for networks to share data, the interconnectivity that enables media convergence and the global reach of information cultures was not in place. So although network protocols do not seem immediately relevant to television or even to using new media today, they are the underlying foundation that allows television networks to share data beamed across satellites, fans to share their critiques and commentary, and new ventures in Internet television like *Hulu* and *Roku* to take place.

The Discursive Formation of Media Convergence

Universal network protocols let a vast array of computers and devices relay information across operating systems—making content the free-floating factor in this moment of media "convergence." Wendy Hui Kyong Chun documents the crucial role of networking protocols to the structure of the Internet in *Control and Freedom: Power and Paranoia in the Age of Fiber Optics*, where she claims "the Internet is a protocol, is TCP/IP" (63).[32] TCP/IP, which refers to Transmission Control Protocol/ Internet Protocol, constitutes the actual "language" rules used by computers to connect to each other across a network. Without shared, universal Internet protocols there would simply be computers and smaller, local networks, and no way to reach across them. Once these protocols were standardized, it became possible to connect a multitude of networks together, a process that gradually led to the emergence of the Internet. Chun's argument, that the Internet is not, as often stated, "a network of networks" but is instead a protocol, a way of communicating, is key to arguments about media convergence. Just as computer and audiovisual technology cannot be linked together if they lack the correct physical connectors and adapters, both technologies must also know how to "talk" to one another, or convergence between them cannot take place. Media content cannot travel across the network without the (software) protocols and (hardware) technology in place that let our PC play a DVD in its drive or our television deliver up its (cable-provided) video on demand.

Media convergence has rapidly become a cottage industry in media and film studies today, where specialists in translation, adaptations, and media industries share their work with those interested in how media products travel across different formal and industrial contexts. By 2010, a growing selection of both academic and media industry conferences dedicated to media convergence has emerged, including Massachusetts Institute of Technology's biennial Media in Transition conference and the University of South Carolina and University of Nevada's co-sponsored Convergence and Society: The Changing Media Landscape, as well as the University of California at Los Angeles and University of Southern California's Transmedia Hollywood 2010 conference organized by Denise Mann and Henry Jenkins. Scholars blog about convergence, and consortiums study its emergence and transmutations.[33] There are introductory texts on media convergence, such as John Pavlik and Shawn McIntosh's *Converging Media: An Introduction to Mass Communication* (2004), and the peer-reviewed scholarly journal *Convergence: The International Journal of Research into New Media Technologies* was launched in 1995 at the University of Luton (now the University of Bedfordshire) in Great Britain. But in many ways it is too soon to tell if scholarly focus upon convergence is a lasting model for studying media technologies and media cultures or if it is just the latest academic fad and fashion.

Let me be clear here: not all theories of convergence are the same in method, practice, or theory. I am skeptical of claims that too easily or uniformly imagine convergence between and among technologies and users, since each technology has its own specific form and each user has his or her own experiences of that form. These differences of form and experience must complicate our notions of convergence. I believe that it is crucial to reconsider the very notion of "convergence" itself.

WHY NOT CONVERGENCE?

It is crucial, then, to disentangle some of the assumed and seemingly naturalized connections between television, personal computers, and video game systems in order to better understand the relationships between these media forms. For instance, in chapter 1, in order to carefully approach 1970s gaming systems and television, there are certain key questions to ask: what were the connections between television sets, video games, and personal computers during the first home video game craze in the late 1970s? How was the public reception of video games and computers linked to television? And in what ways did these new technologies promise to both remake and reframe TV?

The idea of technological, industrial, and cultural convergence is relevant here and requires some explanation. "Convergence" is one of those techno-buzz words that seems both to emblematize and to mystify new technologies. Yet if we take the idea of convergence seriously, it can be a quite useful way of approaching the field of digital culture/new media studies. One dictionary definition of convergence describes the term as it relates to mathematical, biological, and physiological studies, as well as its common definition as "a point of converging, a meeting place." In each of its subject-specific definitions, convergence is described as a kind of merging of data—be it the establishment of a finite limit in math, the physiological "turning of the eyes inward to focus on an object at close range," or its biological definition as the "similarity of form or structure caused by environment rather than heredity." What all of these definitions share and what is useful here is that this coming together—this merging—results in a new grouping or formation: a new model for understanding previously disparate data or information. It is also crucial to understand gaming, computers, and television by noting that in these scientific fields, convergence describes preexisting formal shifts discovered and analyzed using field-specific methodologies. By using the term "convergence" we risk perpetuating the notion that cross-media configurations are themselves naturally occurring phenomena rather than the result of technological innovation, business strategies, and larger economic and cultural forces.

Other theorists have also noted the cultural and economic shifts leading toward media "convergence." The list of what we might call "convergence theorists" includes Paul Virilio, Siegfried Zielinski, Friedrich Kittler, Henry Jenkins, and Brian Winston, among others. Winston traces out a history of media technologies that connects telegraphy, telephony, radio, television, videocassette recorders, computers, cable and satellite transmissions, and the Internet into a history of technological innovations connected together by their use as communications media.[34] Although Winston does not predict that these technologies will merge, he does make connections between them, and ends by predicting that holographic television will be part of the future of these technologies. Siegfried Zielinski, however, does theorize that visual/media culture is progressing toward "advanced audiovision," which will combine the cinematic and the televisual into "a complex kit of machines, storage devices, and programs for the reproduction, simulation, and blending of what can be seen and heard, where the trend is toward their capability of being connected together in a network" (Zielinski 19). Henry Jenkins describes how much of the discourse around convergence relies upon what he has termed the "black box fallacy" that all media will eventually flow through a singular black box into the home. According to Jenkins, "media convergence is not an endpoint; rather, it is an ongoing process occurring at various intersections between media technologies, industries, content, and audiences" (*Convergence Culture* 154). Media use has changed in ways that, as Jenkins tells it, exceed the much-hyped "digital revolution." Jenkins's essay details just how "new media technologies . . . enable consumers to archive, annotate, transform, and recirculate media content" (155). Taking the work of these various theorists of what some now call convergence studies at face value, one concludes that we are just beginning to understand how media and media users come together, and that we can continue to refine scholarship on such occurrences in a wide range of ways.

Media convergence is not in any way inevitable or easy, even if it is presented and packaged and marketed to us as such. Comcast's 2009 "Comcast Town" advertising series portrays these inconsistencies and ruptures in convergence quite convincingly. In the series, the same one-note song is sung by individuals navigating and, in one jingle's title, "Future Hopping" through a *Sim City*–like (1989) complicated imaginary set of public spaces of various anonymous "Comcast Towns," where "Dreaming / bigger/Single cable/One decision/Internet/Phone/Television/ High-speed internet elation/Crazy, fast acceleration." Indeed, Virilio would have a field day with this advertisement, for the occupants of Comcast Town may seem to be partaking in a wide range of digitally enabled, high-speed delights, but they sing in one monotonous voice about the corporate power that makes such digital dreams possible, ending each song with "C-O-M-C-A-S-T!" (see figure 3). This is actually, as many a disgruntled Comcast customer will tell you, the nightmare of media convergence as imagined by capitalism, reminding us (intentionally or not) of Ridley Scott's infamous "1984" advertisement for MacIntosh, which showed drably dressed PC drones listening to the voice of their leader while a sledgehammer-wielding Mac athlete attempts to break them out of their technologically anesthetized state. Perhaps it is good to be skeptical about how, when, and why media convergence is important.

Ultimately, I believe, convergence theory or studies will become a viable approach for academics and media users, just as critical attention to media reception, industry practices, and the distribution/circulation of media have proven to be productive. Although the heyday of "convergence studies" may be just behind us, the specific ways in which media converge and coalesce still have much to tell us. So, too, we can look to the historical models of media convergence, those examples that predate or overlap with the digital era, for a deeper understanding of how the present moment of convergence emerged.

3. Still image from the 2009 Comcast advertisement "Future Hopping."

How Television Is New Media

When assembling their exhaustive anthology *The New Media Reader* (2003), Noah Wardrip-Fruin and Nick Montfort took a long historical look at what constitutes "new media" and included several selections from the deep history of computer technology and its cultures. Among these, notably, is the now-classic exchange between Hans Magnus Enzensberger and Jean Baudrillard about broadcast media, its consumers, and producers, which was originally published in 1971 and 1972 as "Constituents of a Theory of the Media" and "Requiem for the Media," respectively. Passionately arguing in a post-1968 mode, both Enzensberger and Baudrillard call for a radical rethinking of how the "media" (radio, television) should work. They just differ on what they consider radical. Enzensberger calls upon passive consumers to rise up and become producers of the media: "For the first time in history, the media are making possible mass participation in a social and socialized process, the practical means of which are in the hands of the masses themselves. . . . In its present form, equipment like television or film does not serve communication but prevents it. . . . Every transistor radio is, by the nature of its construction, at the same time a potential transmitter" (262). In Enzensberger's model, television and radio as electronic media have an inherent but inert technological capacity to act as a circuit of and for communication, with room within the circuit for participation by once-passive consumers. It would be too easy to simply see Enzensberger as the structuralist socialist theorist, calling for a reversal of roles within the media system. Instead, he reminds his readers in 1970 that the media "demands interaction" (273).

Baudrillard's critique of Enzensberger is direct and cutting, and also emerges out of both structuralism and socialism. For him, it is not enough for one to just learn and adopt the codes of the media oneself. Instead, he calls for a scrambling of signals, a rethinking of the meanings that have been inherited and for a model of the media based on interaction and simulation: "Network-like communications models built on the principle of reversibility of circuits might give new indications of how to overcome this situation" (286). Using computer and cybernetic terms ("network-like," "circuits") as metaphors, Baudrillard hopes to remap the media system as a media network, a set of circuits that can be manipulated throughout their varied processes in an effort to rework the producer/consumer dialectic.

One of Baudrillard's key examples, graffiti, is especially useful in understanding the nuances of his argument. As he puts it, graffiti "simply smashes the code. . . . It [graffiti] works through the instantaneous deconstruction of the dominant discursive code. It volatizes the category of the code, and that of the message" (287). Here Baudrillard describes the discourse of the media as a *code* with an embedded message, echoing McLuhan, whom he mentions throughout the essay as both a model and a flawed theorist of the media. So for Baudrillard, one must both take up the media code and then remake it into a transgression against its sender, the media industry.[35]

Both Enzensberger and Baudrillard provide us with useful tools for understanding new media—and especially for understanding television *as* new media. From Enzensberger we can adopt practices that require us to rethink our positions within and among new media systems. And from Baudrillard we can unlearn the ways we have learned to imagine media, technologies, and systems. One must unlearn how one approaches television—a medium so abstract and banal that at times it has seemed unapproachable—in order to approach television's role in the invention of new media. At the same time, one must contend with media networks that are now reliant upon simulation as their bread and butter and in which interaction is both ever-present and undertheorized. As Professor Brian Oblivion, David Cronenberg's homage to McLuhan in his 1983 film *Videodrome*, said, "Television is reality and reality is less than television." This is true more than ever today, in our new media age.

So, in the early 1970s, Baudrillard and Enzensberger sought to reimagine television's cultural role, each in different ways. In the early 2000s, Wardrip-Fruin and Montfort reprinted this discussion in the interest of establishing an exhaustive anthology of sources that describe and define what we now know to be new media. Before there was new media there was television, raising many of the same critical, cultural, and formal issues. Yet television's invention of new media goes beyond being a mere predecessor to the next new thing in communication, information, media. No, television technology finds its place within early new media technologies—acting as a monitor for proto-personal computer devices and early video games, as discussed in chapter 3. Television is literally connected to new media—to its history and its future. The conclusion of this book explores the physical, tangible connections between television and new media technologies as demonstrated by systems that enable embodied virtual interactions with interactive video in order to complicate our understanding of media convergence and the implied inevitability that contemporary media moves through networks and devices and is made meaningful via fans and consumers as both product and culture.

Television is the crux—culturally and technologically—of this investigation into new media and how we use, imagine, and play with those technologies and objects we group under the domain of "new media." Television—as a medium capable of containing and reframing other media discourses such as radio and film, and as electronic technology that is most aptly set to "converge" with computer technologies—provides the discursive terrain for this investigation. Yet television as a content delivery device continues to take shape in the cultural imaginary as both a specter of low culture's failings and as an almost impossible-to-contain stream of imagery, noise, and discourse. As discursive terrains go, TV is fairly slippery. But it is precisely this slipperiness that makes television ever more "relevant" to discussions of "new media," for television remains a new medium sixty years after its public debut.

Throughout this book television takes on several different forms—just as this term often conjures up a wide range of content, technologies, and experiences. Chapter 2, "Is This Convergence?; Postnetwork Television, New Media, and Emerging Middletexts" explores three specific media convergence case studies from recent years—*South Park*'s (1997–present) "Make Love Not Warcraft" episode, *Dr. Horrible's Sing-Along Blog* (2008), and the ABC Family series/comic book *The Middleman* (2008). In each of these instances, the medium of television is a key aspect of the media product in question, though how "television" is part of the meaning of each work changes from one to the next. Television is a crucial point of signification for all three cases, whether as the medium through which content is delivered (*South Park*) or as the temporarily shut-down industry that enabled the new media production of *Dr. Horrible's Sing-Along Blog*, or as one platform used to bring the transmedia narrative of *The Middleman* to audiences. Through these disparate objects, some common themes emerge: that convergence is the result of a range of industrial pressures as well as creative choices, and that the medium of television provides a sort of map for how the new medium of the Internet can be utilized.

Chapter 3, "From Tube to a 'Series of Tubes': Television in and as New Media" examines the "transmedia" and "intermedia" contact between television and new media (as forms, industries, and technologies). By examining the literal and rhetorical connections made between television and computer technologies, it is possible to discern the varied ways in which television has been *more* than simply a predecessor to new media and is instead a cultural force that helps shape the ways in which the "new" is imagined.

The last chapters of *How Television Invented New Media* concentrate primarily upon uses of new media, television, and video, specifically how video game and computer game systems allow users to play in and on their TV or computer screens.[36] In chapter 4, "ALT-CTRL: The Freedom of Remotes and Controls" the ways that video gaming and play, as well as televisual interactivity through remote controls, can "leak" outside the set and onto real space and real bodies are explored through a discussion of agency, interactivity, and the widespread use of remotes and controllers. Through a consideration of television's history, its technological structures and its continued "convergence" with new media forms and content, *How Television Invented New Media* complicates our understanding of new media and both its origins and futures. The book concludes with an examination of video screens designed for physical interactivity in conjunction with new modes of branding and advertising. These screens, which consumers stand, step, and jump upon, take video and gaming representations together and yield brief encounters with embodied virtuality, while still retaining the window of the screen and the logic of editing and mise-en-scène inherited from television, cinema, and interactive media.

This introduction has traced how television invented new media across a range of discourses—academic, industrial, and popular—and a range of devices such as television sets, personal computers, and computer networks, to name just a few. In doing so, it is possible to see how seemingly disparate modes like convergence studies, video game theory, and the history of new media are all actually part of a larger argument about television and new media as historically linked discourses, as sites through which media crosses over, is translated, and "converges" among. The everydayness and ubiquity of both personal computers and television means that one has to carefully disentangle the meanings that collapse upon objects and devices that broadcast, network, and "stream" media around the clock. Each of the following chapters will approach how television invented and invents new media from a specific angle, considering how television has served as an entry point for computers into the home, interrogating the trope of convergence across industries and representations, and then analyzing convergence through devices designed to literally connect televisions and computers. Video game systems and their discourses of control and interaction point toward an alternate model for thinking of television's place in new media discourse.

CHAPTER 1

"This Is Intelligent Television"

THE EMERGING TECHNOLOGIES OF VIDEO GAMES, COMPUTERS, AND THE MEDIUM OF TELEVISION

"Do your homework while you're watching TV. Basic Math is Atari's first educational Game Program. Solve addition, subtraction, multiplication, and division problems on your own TV. The computer lets you know if you're right. . . . Basic Math. The fun way to learn."

—Atari Video Computer System
1978 catalogue

FROM VIDEO GAMES TO PERSONAL COMPUTERS

This chapter's title is taken from an advertising campaign for Mattel's Intellivision, a home video game system that was first launched in 1979–1980. When writing about gaming, television, and computers, I could not resist Mattel's slogan, which simultaneously encapsulates the bad object status of television and promotes the game system as an engaging and cultured alternative to watching reruns (figure 4). Mattel's print and television advertisements for the system, which starred erudite pundit George Plimpton, sought to brand the Intellivision as a thought-provoking, "smart" video game system, something that current advertisements for Nintendo's *BrainAge* series (2005–2007) continues to do in our era. Although

Intellivision was released later than most of the systems discussed in this chapter, the system and its promotional campaign perfectly demonstrate the rhetorical morass that early video game systems were caught in when making both figurative and literal connections between television, gaming, and computers. And it is these connections—between discrete media formats that share certain commonalities (most notably, a screen)—that I am concerned with here. For rather than theorize a particular genre, mode of interactivity, or process of identification, I suggest we look more closely at actual video game systems—as media apparatuses, as sites of representation, and as the starting points for what scholars today now refer to as "media convergence," a model I explored at length in the introduction. Video games are not often examined within television studies, despite being primarily encountered upon TV. This chapter brings the study of video games into the context of television as it is understood academically.

Computers, video games, and digital media are often part of the same set of conversations, but in these conversations the medium of television is usually only given passing consideration as, quite literally, a "medium" through which this other, newer media "flows."[1] Television's role in digital media history, especially its place in the historical development of digital entertainment technologies such as video game systems and computers, should be emphasized and understood as crucial to new media history and theory. For the then-new technologies of the 1970s, such as the personal computer and video game, television lent more than a basic display apparatus; instead, one finds that the literal links between TV sets and (home or video game) computers were established in relationship to the cultural baggage already associated with television by that time.[2] We can see the way television and video games were imagined together in an illustration from the 1982 Atari catalogue (see figure 5). Centered in the image and hovering above an Atari Video Computer System, a television set displaying a *Pac-Man* (1979) start screen is the destination for rows of games streaming toward it. Underneath, the Atari system rests atop a *Tron*-style (Lisberger, 1982) white grid on a black background.

4. Mattel Intellivision, circa 1979. Note the multigenerational family gathered around the Intellivision console.

The message is clear—together TV and Atari can offer numerous routes toward interactive fun—and these routes are envisioned as excitingly high tech and futuristic.

Often lauded as a "breakthrough" period for television programming and technologies—with the emergence of PBS, "quality" situation comedies, and the rise of cable—television in the 1970s was also understood as a time of cheap formats and exploitative series that former FCC chair Newton Minow had dubbed the "vast wasteland" of TV in 1961.[3] Such a repositioning of television programming as a site of cultural detritus has crucial theoretical ramifications for the history and theory of video games, because such a negative understanding of television contributes to a misunderstanding of TV viewing as unthinking, passive, and déclassé just at the moment that video games emerge as a new and interactive use for the TV medium. Early video game systems expand the TV medium to include television as a framework for gaming, as a technology, and as a space of contact between digital games and gamers. At the same time, Minow's "vast wasteland" logic reinforces a cultural hierarchy that places television viewing below such high-cultural engagements as live

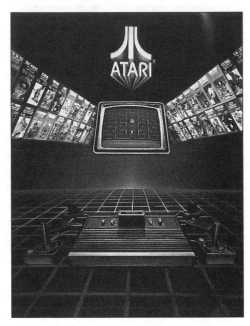

5. 1982 Atari Games
catalogue illustration.

theater and cinema-going. Over time, the assumed passivity of
American television reception, as well as its assumed negative
content, have become naturalized as the way that television
"just is." In *Logics of Television: Essays in Cultural Criticism* (1990),
Patricia Mellencamp writes of the wholesale cultural condemna-
tion of television as a debased medium, claiming that colleagues
who would otherwise consider themselves liberal, culturally
informed humanist scholars still look down upon television as
an object of intellectual analysis (6–7, 12). Mellancamp's obser-
vation, appearing in an early and authoritative anthology of
television scholarship, indicates how easy and acceptable it is
to dismiss television, be it for its "low culture" wares, religious
beliefs, or in favor of more "sophisticated" tastes.

1970s Media Convergence

Although academic interest in media convergence is relatively new (and roughly coincident with the emergence of the
field of new media studies), gamers and computer users have
been practicing convergence for decades as they connect televi-

sions, computers, consoles, speakers, and other media equipment into work/life/entertainment systems.

I should note that, while varying technological components may be merging with one another and have been doing so since the very first oscilloscope/computer game moment, actual media convergence implies that the representations and images produced by each apparatus would also converge.[4] Yet, in the case of television, computers, and gaming, one can use one technology in conjunction with another to produce discrete media forms and experiences—a game or a television program, a spreadsheet, or a game—but typically not both at once.[5] One can now switch between a device's various modes, experiencing the television receiver as television, computer, or game, each with its discrete modes of reception and interactivity. But I cannot *play* an episode of *All in the Family* (1971–1979) with any greater success than I can *watch* a game of *Asteroids* (1979).[6] Instead, the act of switching between these functions becomes a crucial semiotic link, remapping the machine as the screen flashes, blinks, goes black, ready to become my computer and not my television set—at least while I'm playing.[7]

Resetting the Set: Making Television a Game Computer

Much like Steven Johnson's compelling discussion of how video games encourage and activate cognition in *Everything Bad Is Good for You: How Today's Popular Culture Is Actually Making Us Smarter* (2005), my argument is also about how some of the most crucial technological and cultural innovations of video games have largely gone unnoticed while other, more "readable" aspects of gaming continue to garner media attention.[8] What I am not arguing here is that video games are culturally, morally, or aesthetically good or bad.[9] Instead, it is essential to understand how the history of video game systems intersects with the history of television. By understanding the connections between early home gaming systems, TVs, and computers, one can resituate the televisual apparatus within the common historical and theoretical narratives of new media/gaming. Crucial to this discussion is understanding how the boom of the early video game industry brought computers into the home and then connected them (the game system/computer) to the television set during the mid to late 1970s. In many ways the television receiver served as a stable and familiar referent for consumers and users who were first learning to read the semiotics of the new personal computers and video game systems being connected to the more recognizable television set.

The 1980s are widely lauded for the rise of multinational, postindustrial corporations, as well as the widespread use of personal computers in domestic and professional environments and the emergence of the "cultural logic of postmodernism," and the 1970s were when key computing inventions and innovations occurred, in both academic contexts and by individual computing enthusiasts who "homebrewed" their own devices.[10] Developed by early adopters, researchers, and hobbyists, these first personal computers were spectacles as much for what they did as for the very fact of their existence.[11] While the Homebrew Computer Club members were building computers from kits, developments in the leisure industry were leading to some similar innovations.

At the same time that these ostensibly more serious and task-oriented personal computers were being developed, entrepreneurs were producing home gaming systems that attempted to capitalize on the popular 1970s video game arcade trend. Home console games connected to a television set, which was used as the visual display or screen that enabled game play to take place, just as video game systems with external software programs continue to do today. Console games have programs hardwired onto the technology itself, as exemplified by the early Sears Home PONG (1975) manufactured by Atari, and the Magnavox Odyssey (1972). Home gaming systems might include such hardwired games or are programmable "low-level home computers" whose users can swap out cartridges ("carts") to play new games or use ancillary devices to expand the functionality of the gaming system.[12] Contemporary home gaming systems like Microsoft's Xbox 360, Sony's Playstation 3, and the Nintendo Wii all function according to these same technological structures: they plug into the television or "home theater system" directly, and game software is then run off of compact disc or digital video disc media played, using a basic computer in conjunction with stored data such as memory cards loaded with previously saved gameplay (or on-board memory and a hard drive). The user then interacts with the game using a range of input devices like paddles, joysticks, or other handheld controllers. Like the early Atari, Magnavox, Fairchild, Coleco, and Mattel systems produced between 1972 and 1983, contemporary home gaming systems utilize the television receiver as the "gaming computer's" visual display.[13]

TELEVISION'S ROLE IN THE HISTORY OF VIDEO GAMES

Numerous scholars have described how television has become linked with domesticity and subsequently feminized as a domestic, consumptive home "appliance."[14] Typically this view of television as domestic object is used in an analysis of television and gender and the cultural roles TV performs, either through programming or as it is culturally "installed" into specific, gendered spaces.[15] Although this approach to television as domestic appliance has been very productive for the field of television studies, I hope to shift the focus on the domestic uses of television in order to incorporate how televisual domesticity enabled later technologies, like the personal computer, to move from the public, corporate sphere into the private sphere of the home. Such an approach may be counterintuitive within the context of television studies, where the conflation of television with the feminine must now contend with the way that home gaming systems and the literal and figurative connections between television sets and computers require an analysis of television as a device caught up in the construction of a newly masculinized home entertainment zone. Unfortunately, this analysis of the gender politics of television's convergence with games and computers is outside the scope of this project. Instead, we should keep in mind that the "domestication" of any technology will occur in conjunction with other cultural forces, such as the tendency to engender technologies and its uses.

Research and development of home video gaming systems began as early as the mid-1960s (not counting Willy Higinbotham's oscilloscope *Tennis for Two* "video game" displayed in the sole location of the Brookhaven National Laboratory in 1958).[16] In 1968, engineer Ralph Baer applied for the first video game patent (Herman 7) and began to develop the system that would eventually be released as the Magnavox Odyssey in 1972 (Kent 22–26). When Baer began to approach television manufacturers to market and sell his gaming system, he was surprised to find that he had to deal with the public perception that television was for *watching*, not *playing*.[17] According to Leonard Herman's *Phoenix: The Fall and Rise of Home Videogames* (1994), "Baer quickly learned that it wasn't just a simple matter of calling up a television manufacturer and telling them that he had a great new product that would interest them. He first had to make people realize that games *could* be played via a television set and that nothing could go wrong with the television should the player do something wrong" (7). Television was perceived as a mysterious technology, one that brought media into the home but whose internal workings were complex.[18] This perception of television technology as strange and mysterious was a legacy from the first waves of television's domestic postwar popularity, when viewers were unaccustomed to such complex electronic home technologies.[19]

In the mid 1970s, personal computers were more of a dream than a reality. Furthermore, the personal computing industry, which would become a highly competitive market shared by Big Blue (IBM) and the upstarts at Apple Computer, did not yet exist. Computers at that time meant mainframe systems, large computers that were powered by either vacuum tube transistors or the integrated circuit, the landmark design developed in the 1950s and 1960s by engineers at Texas Instruments. Jack Kilby's 1969 "solid state" circuit chip patent and at the military contractor Fairchild Semiconductor (Herman 5, 11) truly revolutionized computers' scale and scope.[20] The integrated circuit technology's compact design would make it the ubiquitous hardware element for a vast range of electronic devices, and its technological architecture enabled the dawning of the "Computer Age." Integrated circuits would allow individual users to play with the component parts of computers, breaking down the large-scale mainframes into increasingly smaller scale tools.

The earliest computer developers and users came out of a community of tinkerers and hobbyists—like the amateur radio enthusiasts who helped advance that technology during its early stages of development. These proto-computer geeks met regularly and shared knowledge about computer hardware and software, perhaps most famously at the Homebrew Computer Club in the San Francisco Bay area. There, wunderkind Steve Wozniak and his savvy partner Steve Jobs debuted the Apple Computer. This first open-box, "open source" community of computer users was a group who shared highly specialized knowledge with one another—early computing clubs and communities were not for those who wanted a "plug and play" experience or for the idly curious. By the mid 1970s, computers were not yet a consumer technology. Ultimately, the iconic stories told about personal computing history lionize groups like the Homebrew Computer Club, the "little guys" who would face off against IBM and other large corporations interested in these emerging technologies. Usually, the stories told about the invention of the PC go something like this: Apple's Wozniak and Jobs develop the key interface and design, borrowing from plans abandoned by researchers at Xerox Parc; Bill Gates finds ways to make computers functional and then creates an alliance between his then-young software company and IBM, the company that ultimately underwrites the large-scale development and manufacture of personal computers with an eye toward the business rather than home market. In 1984, when Apple launched its Apple II and Microsoft released its Windows 1.0 operating system, computers were understood as groundbreaking technologies for both work and leisure—and games were widely available—having already gone through multiple generations of hardware and software development.

When Atari's breakthrough Sears Home PONG console was released in 1976, consumers were ready to play with and on their TVs. This shift toward seeing the television as a playable consumer device is crucial. Although the histories of both computing and mass media contain important contributions from amateurs and hobbyists, the widespread public acceptance and use of home video game systems by a broader audience indicates that consumers were rethinking television's role as a home technology in the mid-1970s. Gaming systems at this time were proto-computers, hardwired to play certain games, and were often promoted in connection with promised future features that would allow the systems to function as personal computers with keyboards and other input devices. When Atari released its Video Computer System (VCS) in 1976, one could approach television both as part of a larger entertainment system and as an interactive "computer." At the same time, network television programming was in the midst of its own shift in cultural rhetoric, with the appearance of socially relevant "quality" television programs and televisual events like the Norman Lear and MTM sitcoms and the miniseries *Roots* (1977). Using today's parlance, we might say that television, as a technology and cultural institution, was in the midst of an "extreme makeover" during the latter part of the 1970s. By being able to repurpose television receivers with add-on technologies like video gaming systems, one could literally transform the television set, turning it into a computer or, more precisely, a computer peripheral.

This shift in attitudes toward TV technology was largely on a conceptual level—part of an imagined nexus of home connectivity that did not yet exist at that time. We see this even in the naming of Atari's system. Video game historian Leonard Herman notes, "Although it has the word *computer* in its name, the VCS was not a computer in the fullest sense. The only thing that console could do was play games with the insertion of a cartridge. It had no other practical purpose" (27). Practicality, utility, and function eventually became defining elements of personal computers, while the leisure-based and nonutilitarian "toy" aspects of interactive digital devices that connected to visual displays would become elided with video game systems and the nascent gaming industry. As Charles Bernstein has noted, video games can be understood as a specific kind of computer, one that is "neutered of purpose, liberated from functionality."[21] This division of work/computer and play/video games quickly became entrenched. Yet there were overlaps between gaming systems and personal computers on many fronts—perhaps most notably in the employment of computing entrepreneurs Steve Jobs and Steve Wozniak at Atari, where, under Nolan Bushnell, the two raised funds for their garage-based Apple company by designing early Atari games like *Breakout* (1976). So, literally, video games were a technical and economic starting point for the personal computer industry.

The history of 1970s and early 1980s home video game systems—usually labeled by fans through reference to the "generations" of hardware in a system—is riddled with domestic technologies that promised to do more than simply play games.[22] Instead, these systems were sold as high-priced toys that might also be linked to other, more "productive" activities like writing, coding, or playing music. Although this is speculation based on my research, I believe that video game and toy manufacturers were anxious about the relatively high cost and potentially limited replayability of their devices, so promises were made about add-on features that were rarely developed in order to justify the high price of a gaming system. Likewise, the connotation of games or toys could be improved through an association with computers and educational technologies.[23] In the first decade of the video game industry's commercial penetration into the home market, gaming companies also produced home computer models, most notably the Atari 400 and 800 PCs and the Colecovision version of the company's ADAM home computer (DeMaria and Wilson 52).

The list of video game systems with promised or realized computer elements is long. It includes the Mattel Intellivision's keyboard component that was eventually scrapped, the Atari 400 and 800 line of 8-bit computers, the Magnavox Odyssey2 with its alphanumeric keyboard (1978), the Colecovision ADAM (add-on parts for the gaming system and stand-alone computer versions were produced), Sega's SC-3000 (computer) version of its SG-1000 video game system (1983), as well as the SG-1000 Mark II (a 1984 Japanese release), a game system with a keyboard.[24] Later Sega also licensed their Mega Drive/Genesis hardware for inclusion in the Mega PC produced by Armstead and marketed it as a home gaming computer in 1992–1993 for a European/U.K. market. Microsoft's 2001 Xbox entry into the video game market significantly included a hard drive, Ethernet networking capabilities, and "all in one" features that blur the distinctions between gaming system, home theater/entertainment system, and computer, turning the software giant into a new player in the hardware business.[25] These system designs indicate an industrywide investment in framing gaming systems in relation to both computers and television. As German media theorist Siegfried Zielinski has declared, these efforts were "an expansion of the traditional television experience" in which television receivers and, eventually, dedicated computer monitors, were "new perception surfaces" for "the interface of man and media-machine" (228). Atari's efforts to link gaming, computers, and television are an instructive example of how such multimedia efforts played out for both the new video game industry and its customers.

Candy and Colleen: The Atari Line of Personal Computers

In this history of now mostly forgotten gaming computer systems, I want to foreground Atari's efforts to produce computers for the domestic market during the 1970s, largely because Atari's eventually failed home computers were designed with television in mind (see figure 6). The systems were configured to hook up to a television receiver and use it as a monitor, much as home video game systems still do today. Atari's 400 ($499) and 800 ($999), also known by the internal nicknames Colleen and Candy (after two Atari employees), were 8-bit computers—the 400 had a membrane keyboard and had less RAM (16K) than the more functional 800, with its typewriter-style keyboard and 48K of RAM. Both were released with ancillary technologies such as a disk drive, datassette drive, and dot-matrix printer (Herman 37). The 400 and 800 were able to display better graphics than Atari's VCS, and the company released several games for the systems but on cartridges that were incompatible with the VCS (Herman 37). Like Atari's earliest home consoles, the 400 and 800 were sold primarily

6. Atari 400 home computer and software. The system assumes that a television receiver will serve as monitor. (Photograph by the author.)

at the company's retail partner, Sears, which had mandated the production of the cheaper 400 machine (Herman, Appendix A "Computers"). The Atari computers competed in the marketplace against video game systems and similarly designed early PCs, such as those produced by Texas Instruments, Radio Shack, and Commodore. As seen in figure 7, computer companies like Commodore produced personal computers such as the Commodore 64 model that was also designed with the (sold separately) television-set-as-monitor setup in mind.

The Atari 400 and 800's computer/television receiver configuration and the accompanying constraints that the Federal Communications Commission places upon television technology (as well as the limitations of that technology itself) framed the personal computer apparatus in a specific, televisual way. They also affected how competitive the Atari units could be against companies like Apple, who did use dedicated computer monitors as displays. Apple Computer's monitors were exclusively designed to display digital content, unlike television sets that were repositioned and repurposed as monitors. Atari's line of computers, like

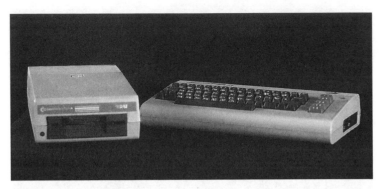

7. The Commodore 64, released in 1982, was a home computer that used the television set as monitor. (Photograph by Colin Johnson, used with permission.)

other "multifunctional" gaming/computer devices produced at the time when personal computers first began to be marketed as consumer products (Is it a computer? A game?), caused customer confusion over which device one should purchase. Marketed as computers and games for average users, these systems appeared to have added value and could potentially bring the esoteric art of programming into the home.

One Atari advertising slogan for the 400 and 800 told consumers, "You don't have to be a genius to use one," playing up the ease-of-use of these home computers. The 400 and 800 systems stand as examples of cross-purposed devices—they are the best version of neither a gaming system nor a computer. As Nintendo of America president Minoru Arakawa said of Coleco's similar ADAM line of dual-use computer/game systems: "It [the Coleco ADAM] was a big mess. How do you define the line between computer and video games? We had a difficult time trying to satisfy both of them" (DeMaria and Wilson 97). In the case of Atari's 8-bit computers, the company did not try to separate out computer and gaming functions. Leonard Herman notes that the release of certain games "cemented the position of the Atari 400 and 800s as a deluxe home arcade machine that was also capable of productivity and business tasks" (Herman A-2). These cross purposes were depicted in advertising that framed the systems as part of a larger discourse about familial, domestic technologies that could bring families together around the machine, reiterating the "family circle" notions first circulated about television in the late 1940s (Spigel, *Make Room for TV* 43–44). Advertisements, game catalogs, system manuals, and other documents depicted multigenerational groups of users huddled around the television set using the new Atari devices, echoing the advertising rhetoric of the 1950s that positioned families around the television receiver, placing the technology at the center of the domestic discourse. Now such home spaces were reimagined as sites of play and work, made possible by the presence of the computer in the home. This new technology promised to be a nexus for family bonding and shared experiences in the realms of play, education, and household management, with Grandpa cheering Junior on as he attempted to achieve a high score (see figure 8).

This approach toward television as an expanded site of work and play was also used for systems more clearly marked

8. Software package for *Basic* (1979) for the Atari 400. (Photograph by the author.)

and marketed for gaming. In 1978 Atari ran a series of television advertisements that starred major athletes of the day, each paired with sports games. Pete Rose and Kareem Abdul Jabaar told their fans, "Don't watch television tonight, play it!" These spot ads, for Atari games like *Home Run* (1978) and *Basketball* (1978), closed with a shot of the television set crowned by the Atari VCS, which was perched on top of it as the add-on that remade the set into a game platform. The athletes' endorsement of the games and encouragement to play rather than watch TV reimagines both the set and its viewers as part of an interactive entertainment discourse.

TELEVISION AND
NEW MEDIA STUDIES

From a strictly technological standpoint, television is closer to the computerized components of digital media culture than cinema is. Television receiver screen size and orientation and computer monitor size and orientation are similar to one another, largely because they rely upon similar technologies— first the cathode ray tube and later the liquid crystal display.[26] As stated earlier, many early personal computing technologies were first manufactured to connect to existing televisual technologies, turning the television receiver itself into a computer monitor. We can also note the way that projected cinematic images differ from the scanned images seen via a cathode ray tube or on a contemporary computer or televisual display. By situating the personal computer as a device accessible through the TV screen, this strategy of TV-as-monitor, born out of the pragmatic and financially motivated ingenuity to retrofit old technology to new, significantly locates computers within popular culture. The TV-as-monitor strategy allowed manufacturers and users of early personal computer systems to inadvertently naturalize the computer as domestic technology with both literal and metaphorical links to television.

This repositioning of television within digital media discourse not only grounds a discussion of the digital in the everyday but it also allows for a reconsideration of television in the home itself. Although outside the scope of this book, these computer-television connections necessitate further study. In particular, as mentioned, we need to rethink accepted notions about the gendered reception of contemporary television, especially in light of the emergence of high-tech domestic home theaters and gamer environments as do-it-yourself home media worlds that complicate the history of separately gendered domestic media/leisure spheres.[27]

As stated at the outset, repositioning the role of television within this analysis has implications for how video game studies and television studies negotiate the very medium of gaming and the spaces in which one games. It also creates a link between video game theory and the field of television studies. Although the ramifications of such a connection are an unanswered question at this point, there are academic advantages to approaching video game theory from a perspective informed by television studies. Television scholars have successfully charted out a field with particular attention to social history, media reception, TV viewership, computer usership, and media politics.[28] Several prominent television scholars, most notably Henry Jenkins, have even morphed into advocates for the study of new media like games and gaming.[29] As points of technological and content-driven convergence continue to increase, understanding how television and its history are embedded within video game culture is ever more critical. Although these early examples of televisions harnessed into home computers give some indication of how one technology helped to create a domestic space for others, it is also important to note more recent attempts—successful or not—to bring computing, gaming, and television together.

Ultimately the discourses of convergence, change, emergence, novelty, and innovation that surround digital media technologies must be tempered with a careful reconsideration of older media technologies such as television and cinema. Without sensitivity to the historicity of media and its experience, seemingly natural comparisons and connections between media emerge as though out of a vacuum. Yes, media do become deeply entwined formally and technologically, but our tales of convergence must be situated in a framework that accounts for each form's specificity and use.

The literal and symbolic connections to media forms that already have established formal qualities, methods of distribution, and models of reception provide an anchor for emergent technologies, a starting point for framing how one plays/uses/works on/interacts with/spatially locates and understands computers and video games as part of personalized, domestic environments. And, although the rhetorically condescending attitude toward television was certainly intentional when Mattel deemed their Intellivision game system "intelligent television," it is crucial to understand how preconceptions about television shore up, serve, and frame both the computer and video game mediums through the strategies I have mentioned here. TV continues to provide a framework for digital media experience in an era when we are told, once again, to engage with "smart TV." Without repositioning television into the history of digital media, one cannot pause in front of and amid the connections between the elements of our digital home media systems to consider the seeming inevitability of digital media platforms and the array of experiences they promise.

In the next chapter, the so-called logic of media convergence is considered through three instances where multiple technologies and industries come together and produce new content emblematic of how television and new media have fruitfully combined, despite and because of changes in media industry labor practices, content distribution, and circulation. Alongside these factors that shape "convergence," one also witnesses the emergence of new visualities informed by both their sites of reception on computer screens and television sets and sites of production in studios and inside computer games.

CHAPTER 2

Is This Convergence?

POSTNETWORK TELEVISION, NEW MEDIA, AND EMERGING MIDDLETEXTS

> I have hacked into your broadcast to tell you
> that television is dead. That's right sofa-
> monkeys, no more "corporate entertainment."
> No more self-congratulatory awards shows
> with athletic yet luminous hosts. The future
> of home entertainment is the Internet. Why
> watch something like this [gestures to the
> wide screen of the high definition television
> broadcast], when you can see it like *this?*
> [Dr. Horrible's screen becomes a small insert
> on the wider television screen]
>
> —Dr. Horrible's "pirate" interruption
> of the 2009 Emmy Awards broadcast,
> September 20, 2009

To further demonstrate how television is central to new media, let us consider three recent texts: the 2006 Emmy-winning episode of *South Park* entitled "Make Love, Not Warcraft"; the 2008 ABC Family series *The Middleman*; and *Dr. Horrible's Sing-Along Blog* (2008), a World Wide Web supervillain-musical series launched online and produced during and in response to the 2008 Writers Guild of America strike. Rather than perform straightforward textual analyses of each of these media texts, I suggest we consider them "tutor texts," following N. Katherine Hayles's methodology around science fiction and science introduced in her book *How We Became Posthuman: Virtual Bodies in Cybernetics, Literature, and Informatics* (1999). Hayles posits that tutor texts can act as lens through which one views cultural problems, such as, in this case, media convergence (22–23, 33). These tutor texts can instruct us in multiple ways: demonstrating how "cultural convergence" takes place in contemporary media, showing how media users navigate and follow stories and their creators across platforms, and providing us with a model of how a new media reception/ production practice such as *machinima* can be recapitulated as part of an original commodity product, via the cross-platform collaboration and industrial labor of television animators working alongside video game animators.[1] In each of these modalities, tutor texts are about more than just convergence. Instead, one sees the intersection of particular hardware and software forms together, and sees shifts in media industry labor practices; one can also see the intersection and overlap of multiple forms of representation—from comics to blogs to public Web forums to television and beyond. Throughout these examples, the medium of television performs a crucial and cohesive role—containing new forms (like machinima) while also providing its "old," established styles and aesthetic to Web serials (as in *Dr. Horrible*) and anchoring new attempts to address audiences via the Web with more familiar programming formats.

PWNED . . . WATCHING THE TV/GAME

In 2006, South Park Studios collaborated with Blizzard Entertainment, the computer games studio behind such popular hits as *Warcraft* (1994), *Diablo* (1997), and *Starcraft* (1998). In the 2000s, Irvine, California–based Blizzard became a leading producer of MMOs—Massively Multiplayer Online games, also known as MMORPGs (massively multiplayer online role-playing games). Blizzard's entries into this fast-growing industry sector are *World of Warcraft* (2004) and its "expansions" (read: sequels) *World of Warcraft: The Burning Crusade* (2007), and *World of Warcraft: Wrath of the Lich King* (2008). *South Park*'s production team approached Blizzard Entertainment out of a desire to depict its school-aged protagonists playing on and in a multi-player computer game environment. Prior tests had shown that effectively creating and animating an original computer game for the television episode was not feasible, so *South Park*'s creators wrote *World of Warcraft* into the episode script.

In the episode's narrative, the four grammar-school aged boys of South Park, Colorado, enthusiastically play *World of Warcraft* until a rogue gamer with an illegal tool repeatedly kills off and humiliates or "pwns" their characters.[2] Determined to beat this gamer and save the world (of *Warcraft*), the boys become abject, stereotypical loser gamers—gaining weight, developing acne, playing the game at all hours until able to take on the villain. In a side plot, Stan's dad Randy desperately tries to bond with his son by also playing the game—going so far as to crash the boy's raiding party as a "nube" or new player. Yet it is Randy who eventually saves the day and obtains the in-game weapon necessary to defeat the rogue gamer and make the *World of Warcraft* a safe realm to play in once again. The story-line moves back and forth between South Park and the game company headquarters in California, where the developers are also concerned that the rogue gamer is destroying the game.

What sets the episode apart is its unique incorporation of video game animation into the story. Borrowing a technique from online game communities, the South Park and Blizzard animators created machinima, or machine-cinema of the game, using the actual game as its own virtual camera. Machinima is made by capturing footage of gameplay and then editing that footage to its own soundtrack. In addition to using machinima footage, "Make Love, Not Warcraft" also incorporates custom footage co-produced by video game and television animators that allowed them to include unique objects, actions, and details into the television episode that are unavailable to gamers in a typical *World of Warcraft* session.[3]

"Make Love, Not Warcraft" opens in a surprising way—the audience hears grand, epic music and sees an establishing shot of a bustling, clearly computer-generated town thoroughfare complete with glowing lanterns, giant oak trees, and a Tudor-style town hall filled with the bustle and travel of numerous citizens. The scene cuts to shot that foregrounds one such resident, a red-bearded, armored Dwarf Paladin bearing a two-handed mace, who runs to the front of the frame. This figure's imposing musculature and weaponry are quickly undercut when we hear him speak and his voice is that of a young, annoying child—for this is *South Park*'s loathsome and self-centered Eric Cartman in his *World of Warcraft* persona. He declares, characteristically, "Oh *dude*! I just took the biggest crap!" Soon Cartman's dwarf meets up with his gaming party, each in species and character class-specific attire—Stan plays a human warrior, while Kyle's character is a comely, buxom red-haired human (female) mage and Kenny is represented by a bulked-up, bow-and-arrow-wielding human hunter (see figures 9 and 10). While these *World of Warcraft* avatars look distinctly different from the boys' typical "construction paper cutout" animated style, each does retain attributes of the character he or she represents, as in the visual match-up of the WoW avatar's gear with the boy's hat or parka, the carry-over of voices between South Park and Azeroth (the world of *World of Warcraft*) via TeamSpeak microphones that allows for the Azeroth characters to sound like the boys and in their logical choices of avatar species and class. (It makes

9. *South Park*'s Stan, Kyle, Cartman, and Kenny inside the realm of Azeroth as represented by their *World of Warcraft* avatars. (Copyright South Park Studios.)

10. Stan, Kyle, Cartman, and Kenny at the school computer lab *South Park.* (Copyright South Park Studios.)

sense, for example, that Eric Cartman's Dwarf wields a huge, oversized mace in light of Cartman's over-the-top, egotistical personality.)[4]

"Make Love, Not Warcraft" was the first American television episode partially shot on location in Azeroth, the virtual world of the *Warcraft* games.[5] The episode also goes beyond simply referencing gaming culture and stereotypes. The show looks like and was made using the actual game and scenes in Azeroth, intercut with scenes in South Park that are animated in the series' usual style, which is visually different; they are edited to productively juxtapose with one another. Because of the way in which machinima footage is captured rather than shot, Azeroth locations in the game world had to be designated and used for the production, and special servers had to be set up to prevent actual gamers from unintentionally wandering into a scene.[6] From the opening shot, when Cartman shouts to his companions, TV viewers see four fantastical game characters rather than a usual episode opening with the four boys. The visual texture and style of this *Warcraft* animation is completely at odds with the show's typical, simplistic 2.5 dimensional look, and this provides the humor. Even elements as simple as character movement—jerky and repetitive in-game while smooth and fluid in South Park, add to the humor, as animation that is acceptable and even considered cutting-edge on the computer screen looks somewhat choppy and stilted on the television screen, even as it retains a superior level of visual detail over South Park's simulated construction-paper world. The ridiculousness of characters repeatedly hopping up and down or breaking out into an impromptu dance—both common and unremarkable inside the game itself—stand out when watched on television. This effect builds as the episode continues and the boys play the game more obsessively, no longer able to have any distance from it as they attempt to "level up" their characters. By the end of the episode, while their *World of Warcraft* avatars have become hugely powerful and can command great forces of magic and weaponry, the boys themselves have become obese, sedentary, and acne-ridden, just like the adult gamer that they have been pursuing. Like many *South Park* episodes, "Make Love, Not Warcraft" both praises and speaks to gamers while critiquing their culture at the same time (see figure 11).

By adopting and translating the machinima aesthetic into a (basic cable) mainstream television format, *South Park*'s creators and animators took an innovative and emergent fan practice and produced with it an innovative half hour of television that was still recognizable as *South Park*—as an animated situation comedy. The machinima aesthetic, which is not easily

11. The mighty MMORPG warriors at school, leveling up their avatars as other children gaze on in disgust. (Copyright South Park Studios.)

reduced and in practice is as varied as its own producers make it, depends upon the juxtaposition of a game world and characters with elements (music, dialogue, action, carefully coordinated gameplay) from outside that world.[7] In "Make Love, Not Warcraft," this is evident in the opening scene, as Cartman's dwarf character runs on-screen declaring that he just "took the biggest crap!" Stan's and Kyle's in-game characters react with the characters' typical responses to such news and in the characters' normal voices, yet those voices are now mapped onto a chain mail–clad warrior and a sorceress in flowing green and gold robes.

In jokes and up- to-the-minute popular culture references abound in "Make Love, Not Warcraft," as they do in most *South Park* episodes. The villainous bad guy Jenkins—an obese, oversized-glasses-wearing geek who spills food on himself as he adjusts his keyboard and mouse while wearing the kind of wrist braces worn by sufferers of repetitive stress injuries— is named after Leeroy Jenkins, perhaps the most "famous" machinima star to date. Jenkins is a machinima character created for a short *World of Warcraft* machinima video spoofing guilds or teams who overplanned and overstrategized their dungeon raids in the game. In the video, Jenkins's guild is carefully planning an attack when "Leeroy" returns to his keyboard after taking a snack break. He storms into the dungeon, shouting "Let's do this! Leeeeeeeeeeeeeeeeeroy Jenkins!!!" and his guild is forced to follow him in and are all swiftly massacred as a result. The video was such a hit online that it spawned parodic advertising by Toyota, mainstream press coverage, and the addition of a "Jenkins" suffix to a characters' name for achieving a particular feat designated by Blizzard.[8] Again, the *South Park* scribes and animators seem to be both inside of the gaming subculture and simultaneously mocking it through the Jenkins character, as underscored by the episode's juxtaposed visual styles and images of heroics matched with those of physically and socially abject losers. We might even say that it is the uneasy disjunction between new media (computer games) and old (television) that provides us with the joke here.

The "translation" of machinima into *South Park* was not an easy one and, in fact, the episode isn't really an exact translation or convergence of machinima and traditional television animation at all. Instead, it might be best to think of it as an example of stylistic convergence and industrial coproduction between computer game and television animators.[9] As South Park Studios technology supervisor J. J. Franzen puts it, "So, we basically ended up with in-game and Maya versions of the exact same characters which allowed us to cut back and forth between in game footage, and footage we animated and rendered ourselves" ("Make Love, Not Warcraft," machinima.com). Franzen's description of the production process calls attention to how the animators both created original footage using the software program Maya and by "shooting on location" in the game itself via the machinima practice of staging game events and capturing footage to edit later. So, "Make Love, Not Warcraft" is actually quite a complex text: stylistically it juxtaposes two distinct forms of animation and production; industrially it brings together game animators and television animators (each of whom are fans of the others); and it is an instance of bringing together old media and new media to produce an innovative television episode that is both a new media and old media object.[10]

This new media/old media dynamic was made even more complex in March 2008, when South Park Digital Studios was launched online as a coproduction between Stone and Parker's South Park Studios and Comedy Central (as backed by the MTVN Entertainment Group, which is in turn a subsidiary of Viacom). South Park Studios, like Hulu and other television-for-the-Internet services, allows users to view free streaming versions of *all* South Park episodes, with new episodes appearing for limited periods of time as determined by the licensing agreement between Comedy Central as the television distributor of *South Park* and South Park Studios as the content creators and online distributor.[11] On the Web site, users can play *South Park* flash games, read a full episode guide for the series, access and download images and sounds from episodes, watch behind-the-scenes special features, or create one's own "mix" of a *South Park* scene, in addition to watching whole episodes or clips from episodes.[12]

The content, like the show itself, ranges from the scatological and juvenile to detailed, "insider" information on the series in its production blog and animation features.[13] Incorporating both the now-standard elements found in network-produced, official Web sites for television programs (clips, still images, chats with producers, and links to related products available for purchase) and elements that fans often produce for each other and share online, like an episode guide or remixed content, South Park Digital Studios appears to be speaking to multiple audiences at once, while also, through the type and vast volume of content made available, making a commentary about how such content should circulate. As Parker and Stone describe their interest in the Web site, "We got really sick of having to download our own show illegally all the time so we gave ourselves a legal alternative" ("South Park Digital Studios Press Release"). In this online incarnation, which calls attention to *South Park* as a cultural production through the site's own name—South Park Digital Studios—one can endlessly wander inside *South Park*'s textual universe. Here, there is no endpoint to media convergence, just perpetual opportunities to consume and remix media.

"OH, PHOOEY!": SEEKING OUT THE MIDDLETEXT

In the summer of 2008, keen to relaunch and rebrand its cable network as one for a "new kind of family,"[14] the ABCFamily television network premiered *The Middleman*, a comic-book-based science fiction series from Emmy award–winning television producer Javier Grillo-Marxuach. From a certain perspective, the marketing and launch of this new program is typical of the contemporary television industry: the show had a Web site with interactive features, posted regular Webcasts and podcasts by the show's creator and actors, and translated its aesthetic—the sights and sounds and style—of the television program onto its Internet Web site. What makes *The Middleman* stand out as emblematic of postnetwork television and, seemingly, of media convergence, is the content itself and its strange migration from speculative film script to independent comic book and then, in another act of transubstantiation, into a television series with a twelve-show commitment from a network.[15]

The Middleman makes an excellent case for testing out how television is the ur-new medium, able to contain and refract various versions, textualities, markets, and forms. Thoroughly postmodern in its self-reflexive, fast-paced dialogue that references everything from obscure James Bond villains, surrealist art, British television, comic books, and the Jerry Lewis oeuvre, *The Middleman* is a show for a specific, niche television audience, and very much in line with ABCFamily's goal to succeed as a demographically driven niche network. The story line was originally developed in the 1990s, and some of Grillo-Marxuach's popular culture references had to be updated for new millennial television—in particular, the lead character of Wendy Watson morphs from a white Generation-Xer into a young Latina woman in the transition from comic book to TV screen.[16] *The Middleman*'s comic book influences are evident in both stylistic and narrative choices—outrageous B-movie monsters, weapons, and sight-gags abound, as do mysterious portals into the underworld, encounters with robots, aliens, Mexican wrestlers, super-intelligent primates, and supermodel succubi. As the promotional poster for the series proclaims, *The Middleman* is "fighting evil so you don't have to" in high-kitsch style, complete with Wendy in a vinyl catsuit and carrying an oversized ray gun while the clean-cut Middleman totes two giant guns and both characters knowingly smirk at the camera (see figure 12).

In *The Middleman*, we see iconographic convergence, in which content and narrative travel across media from comic to television to the Web, and medium-specific iterations of the story.[17] The comic book version of *The Middleman* uses standard comics framing and storytelling devices, just as the televisual version utilizes typical television series and episode story forms like narrative arcs and a four-act episode structure. Within each version, there are shifts in the representation of stories and characters—the comic book Wendy is (visually, performatively) not the television Wendy. These medium-specific differences demonstrate how each medium performs

12. *The Middleman* promotional poster. (Copyright ABCFamily, 2008.)

itself through the producers' approach to the format. Despite the *transmedia* migration of content, the structures that differentiate each medium—be it television or the Web or comics—remain recognizable as narrative and formal signposts, signaling to consumers and media users how to read and understand both the form and the content it delivers. In this subtle use of standardized formal elements within transmedia and convergence culture, television occupies a crucial role. TV brings with it a long history of stylistic forms of address and narrative conventions, all of which can be carried over and reiterated online and elsewhere, rendering the new media more recognizable and readable in the process.[18]

Stylistically, television has also historically occupied a kind of "middle place" in culture—disseminating style, form, and trends while also shaping and developing those same trends. So a comic-book, tongue-in-cheek television version of *The Middleman* is stylistically coherent in a way that a filmic version (lacking the seriality and tone of TV) might not be. *The Middleman* also, quite nicely, makes a good "middle case," as the show revolves around a secret figure and his apprentice who act as go-betweens between the "straight" world and the more zany universe in which comic book monsters and tales are real. What

I argue in the following pages is that, in both this program and others, television itself has become a kind of "middleman" of media—a technology that "glues" together the old and new in terms of style, industry, and technology.

On the industrial level, one can observe how television production happens in conversation with and informed by online media practices in blogs, forums, and video sites. Writers, producers, and show runners engage with or observe their fan base from the vantage point of their computer screens, where they are literally "close" to the words, feedback, and critique of online communities of all sorts—in network-sponsored chats, blog threads, or on fan-produced sites with these same features. Fan chatter becomes another aspect of production, to be measured and taken in along with network notes on scripts, casting, and story arcs: these "networked publics" of the new media sphere are more than simply points of convergence—they are readymade marketing focus groups, volunteering and self-publishing their feedback in communities that serve multiple purposes.[19] Media industry scholar John Caldwell summed up the interconnectedness of the varied participants and components surrounding contemporary media products in his short essay, "Welcome to the Viral Future of Cinema (Television)":

> Each multimedia platform (the Web site and the DVD with extras) serves as a "host body" for the studio/network's mutating content, and various forms of industrial reflexivity (behind-the-scenes, making-ofs, bonus tracks, and interactively negotiated production knowledge) serve as the fuel that drives the endless mutation of this content across proprietary host bodies within the conglomerated world. As a form of constant textual renegotiation, onscreen critical analysis (whether from scholars, publicists, show-biz reports, or industrial marketing departments) facilitates the process of repurposing and mutation. (95)[20]

In other words, how one accesses a media product like *The Middleman* (or most Hollywood film and television today) and how much of the related but "paratextual" content found online and elsewhere one consumes determine what one gets—the comic fan's *The Middleman* is different from the TV viewer's version, as was the version produced by ABCFamily and communicated via the show's Web site.[21] Just as a media narrative's "host body" shifts, so do its iterations and reception. Amid all of this commotion and convergence, new figures emerged as industry stars, the traditionally behind-the-scenes writers and producers of television became increasingly "known" commodities to their Internet-savvy audiences.

In the early 2000s, television networks and fans saw the emergence of a newly recognizable TV persona: program producers or show runners became part of the industry discourse, just as viewers gained access to tools like the Internet Movie Database and were able to learn more about the off-camera personnel and writing talent that worked on their favorite programs. This show-runner-as-star phenomenon is often found in one-hour dramas, where writer/producers like J. J. Abrams (*Alias, Lost*), Joss Whedon (*Buffy the Vampire Slayer*), Aaron Sorkin (*The West Wing*), Amy Sherman (*Gilmore Girls*), and Rob Thomas (*Veronica Mars*) are visibly part of the public discourse surrounding the programs they have written and produce.[22]

Even as the Internet and the World Wide Web have become a "middle place" for television networks and fans, they have also become a vital location for industry professionals to gather and speak to their unseen but active audiences. The embrace by *The Middleman*'s Grillo-Marxuach and other TV scribes (Joss Whedon, Kevin Williamson, Shonda Rhimes, and Rob Thomas, to name just a few) of blogs, forums, and the show-runner-as-star production and (self-)marketing model has allowed for an extension of narrative universes, characters, "behind the scenes" gossip via blogs, social networking sites, fan forums, and other sanctioned and unsanctioned zones of online televisual discourse.

Posts like the infamous *Buffy the Vampire Slayer* (1997–2003) "fairy tale" by fired stunt coordinator Jeff Pruitt, as well as live talks with episode scribes and show runners have became part of the extratextual, extramedial culture surrounding television programs and networks.[23] Extratextual elements—those coming from outside of the narrative world of a media product, be

it a program or film, such as the knowledge of a key actor's
other roles—are still caught up in how such narratives are both
exhibited and received by the public, and fandom scholars
have gone to great lengths to describe the ways that the extratextual imparts meanings to texts.[24] Meanwhile, paratextual
elements such as marketing materials, trailers, teasers, and the
like produce versions of a text and its worlds that also contribute
to a narrative's overall coherence or, as in some media franchises,
incoherence. What may have emerged as a newfound way for
producers, writers, and networks executives to monitor public
interest in a program in the mid-1990s, when Usenet groups
and fan forums were flourishing as part of the pre-Web Internet,
has become a standardized part of how shows are marketed to
audiences.

Today one can read a "character's" blog for shows like *How
I Met Your Mother* (2005–present), *The Office* (2005–present),
and *Entourage* (2004–present) or participate in live discussions
with media makers on a regular basis, particularly during highly
promoted viewing periods like "sweeps" in July, November,
February, and May each year, when advertising rates are set and
viewership measured via ratings is most meaningful to those
in the business of television. Here the Internet is an important
ancillary space for addressing, finding, and building audiences.
Television producers and network executives craft shows that
appeal to not just demographically "niche" audiences but also
to both tech-savvy and non-tech-savvy audiences.[25] In the
American television industry of the 2000s, "transmedia" content
production is an early, important part of the pre-production
process for some producers, like those who have worked to
build and incorporate mobile episodes (mobisodes) that run in
parallel to a series, as in *Lost* (2004–2010) and *Battlestar Gallactica*
(2004–2009).[26] Although *The Middleman* was not considered a
successful television program, the series did build the overall
audience for *Middleman* content now available as comics, online,
and a DVD box set. In this regard, it remains more than just
a one-off summer series, and lives on in its other transmedia
forms and fan-distributed clips circulating on FunnyorDie.com,
YouTube, and other online video sites. *The Middleman*'s tele-

visual failure amid its ongoing and long online incarnation demonstrates the ways that sometimes audiences and content *do not* converge—at least not in the ways one expects them to. Nearly a year after the series' cancellation, the entire cast of *The Middleman*, having moved on to other series, networks, and film projects, gathered at the 2009 San Diego Comic-Con to do a table-read of the series' final, unaired episode, which is (of course) included in its DVD box set. As *Arrested Development* (2003–2006) executive producer Mitchell Hurwitz told one reporter in 2005, "you know, in a funny way we often feel that we're really making a show for the new technology here. We're making a show for TiVo and we're making a show for DVD and it really becomes, you know, part of our objective in making this thing, particularly now that we see that, all right, these numbers are kind of staying where they are and yet the DVDs appear to be selling pretty well."[27] Clearly, according to Hurwitz at least, "television" and what constitutes it, as well as what it will become, is changing in light of both new media and convergence. "Television" is no longer just what is broadcast or distributed via cable to TV receivers—it extends to the Web, to DVDs, and to other points of consumption. In the next example, the actual production of media rather than how audiences find and use it becomes the starting point for convergence.

CONVERGENCE AND INDUSTRIAL PRESSURES: BELABORING NEW MEDIA FORMS

The 2007–2008 television season was most notable for what it was not: a complete television season. Instead, a labor dispute and subsequent strike by the Writers Guild Association shut down television production and shortened the seasons (and in some cases completely eliminated the television season, as with Fox's apocalyptic terrorist caper *24*). Actors, writers, and crew members were suddenly without work. In the midst of this unexpected creative labor downturn, Web productions (non-union, of course) flourished. Judd Apatow, Will Ferrell, and Adam McKay's site *Funny or Die*, which uses social recommender systems to rank content so it is either high-

lighted or "dies," continued to post short films produced by and
starring Hollywood writers and stars. And television producer
Joss Whedon, an early adopter of online communications with
fans, put together a professional cast and crew to make *Dr.
Horrible's Sing-Along Blog*, a three-part "supervillain musical"
made explicitly for the World Wide Web and then later released
both via Apple's iTunes online store and DVD.

Critically lauded and notable for its distinctive style that
combined signature Whedonesque elements (genre blending, the
sung-through musical with original score) with an intentionally
"online" serial style, *Dr. Horrible* was a singular instance of televisual and online convergence of content, production, and form.[28]
The series' online style was connoted both by its episodic video
blog style, commonly seen on YouTube, and by its particular
comedic traits and references. When Neil Patrick Harris's Dr.
Horrible practices his evil laugh and then rambles on about
cumin, reading fan emails and describing the strength of his
application to the Evil League of Evil in front of his webcam
that "films" the series, dressed in an old-fashioned medical tunic
and wearing lab goggles, he epitomizes the stereotypical delu-
sionally self-important nerd blogger (see figure 13). The series'
musical numbers also play along youth-oriented "loser" and
comic book themes ranging from going to the Laundromat, the
nobility as well as thanklessness of charity work, and the need
for a freeze ray to stop the world. *Dr. Horrible's* world seems like
a mirror of everyday life, but it is also a world in which the
villain is the actual hero of the piece, a guy who uses an iPhone
application to remotely drive a van but can't get up the courage
to talk to his Laundromat crush, while the knuckleheaded hero,
Captain Hammer, is obsessed with his "hair blowing in the
breeze" and how "this is so nice/I just might sleep with the
same girl twice."

San Francisco Chronicle television critic Tim Goodman noted
the television/Internet synergy and *Dr. Horrible* in particular in
his year-end roundup, where he grouped *Dr. Horrible's* innovation with the development and launch of Hulu.com, the
online site that distributes both first-run and "classic" television, previously discussed in chapter 1. Goodman writes: "*Oh,*

13. Neil Patrick Harris as Dr. Horrible.

yeah, the Internet: Although we thought the Internet-will-kill-television stories all dried up in 2006 from lack of proof, there were at least three noteworthy TV-related developments. First, Joss Whedon's *Dr. Horrible's Sing-Along Blog* proved that with a great TV writer, some fine TV actors, and some TV-quality video, a real phenomenon could arise in otherwise lean times. Second, Hulu.com continued to be relevant, and that forced most networks and cable channels to improve their own sites, which is development No. 3."[29]

Both Hulu and *Dr. Horrible* are examples of how the changing business of television in the United States has utilized the Internet as a new site of content distribution and the circulation of a brand—be it a network brand or the sign of a TV "auteur" like Whedon. In fact, in 2008 the American Film Institute recognized *Dr. Horrible's Sing-Along Blog*, the only online entertainment product noted in its report, as a "moment of significance" for its role "in the evolution of established artists presenting short films online" (Kilday). The business model for *Dr. Horrible* included both new and old media revenue streams and was tied to the concept of Web liveness and simultaneity—the series was initially released for free and in three parts, after which the series then went to iTunes, where viewers could pay-to-view the entire saga or download the songs like a soundtrack album. A later DVD release was also planned from the start (Whitney). Yet in discussing *Dr. Horrible*, it is important to remember that one reason why it works as "convergence" media is its high-quality production values. Like Hulu, which signifies its high quality through both the content it delivers and the quality of its streaming media, *Dr. Horrible* is a "quality" piece of media: well written and acted, it's a funny send-up of superhero genre conventions, a series where one could cheer on Neil Patrick Harris's supervillain wannabe, all the while aware that this was online media produced to Hollywood production standards by actual Hollywood professionals "freed" from their day jobs by a labor dispute (some might even see this "horrible" project as a form of strike-breaking). *Dr. Horrible*, with its studio-quality production values, has adopted the codes of online "imperfect cinema," a term that Henry Jenkins adapted from Third Cinema in order to describe how amateur Web media works use parody to mask technical imperfections (Jenkins, *Convergence Culture* 286). Yet in *Dr. Horrible*, parody is not necessary to mask a lack of professional production values, which are maintained. Instead, *Dr. Horrible* deploys parody of generic conventions for its own stylistic purposes—further marking it as an online series. Here the "amateur" strategy utilizing parody and a seemingly "less polished" look, both contained within the narrative itself as Dr. Horrible's "homegrown" supervillain operation, are recognizable and readable as a new media style. Neither parody nor amateurism is inherent in the piece, but each is instead adopted as a representational strategy for what it signifies for its audience.

In 2004, William Boddy's *New Media and Popular Imagination* took on a wide range of attempts to digitize television—from interactive TV to WebTV to digital video recorders and high-definition television broadcasting and legislation. Boddy quotes CNET reporter Ian Fried's 2001 claim that "the dream of combining PC technology with America's favorite entertainment medium has become a nightmare" (Fried as quoted in Boddy 137). Indeed, Boddy goes on to predict, "If the long-heralded convergence of personal computer and TV set indeed ever comes about, it will not be without leaving a formidable number of major corporate causalities and junked business plans in its wake" (137). Yet, as Boddy indicates later in his text, such test cases, failures, one-offs, and even early successes like "Make Love, Not Warcraft," *The Middleman*, and *Dr. Horrible's Sing-Along Blog* are productive and instructive moments in the emergence of the technologies themselves and the ways that users normalize and codify those technologies.[30]

In these examples, we can clearly see that television *is* a part of new media cultures such as online game worlds, blogs, fan forums, and video sites, and as the place where television creators and actors go to play, perform, and comment on the industry itself. The Internet remains a site for creative experimentation and a zone for frank and detailed discussions of how media gets made and distributed. While writing this chapter, I decided to retrace earlier research I had done about labor disputes on the set of *Buffy the Vampire Slayer* back in the late 1990s. Although in 2009 I could not easily find official historical documents or even industry coverage of these events a decade after they occurred, I was not surprised to find that fans of the show continued to archive their debates and discussion on the issue, and were even advising present-day users and new fans to go back and check specific dates in the online archives to increase their knowledge of the show and its production. Ever "new" in its appearance and use by each successive generation of computer-savvy individuals, the Internet is now also able to provide something resembling historical context, especially when it comes to television shows where watching, recapping, building episode guides, and reviewing have become part of the television culture itself, on sites like Television Without Pity and BuddyTV. com. It is far too late to try to separate the middletext of television out of new media or vice versa—and that should not come as a surprise. Television has been hard to contain—to keep discrete—from its very beginning. In a passage about television that always makes me smile, theorist Richard Dienst argued that those seeking to understand television view it as a problematic rather than an object, for, "Although the term 'television' seems specific in a way 'capitalism' and 'modernity' (not to mention 'postmodernity') do not, it definitely belongs to the same plane of abstraction, the same scope of materiality, and hence the same theoretical hesitation" (3). Once not even a comprehensible or productive term, as abstract as capitalism, television is now a grounding figure and point of reference for new media. But, as "Make Love, Not Warcraft," *The Middleman*, and *Dr. Horrible* all show, television is not just a historical referent for new media, it is also a constitutive force in its formation. Sometimes, as chapter 3 argues, television is integral to the formation of the "new," as in the rhetoric of television online and in conjunction with computers. Furthermore, the very qualities often elided with the new—speed, liveness, interactivity, and connectivity—can all be associated with television first. TV was the "tube" long before there was an Internet or a YouTube. In these ways then, television is part of new media, just as it was in 2006, when South Park producers approached Blizzard Entertainment developers to help make their "crossover episode."

CHAPTER 3

From Tube to a
"Series of Tubes"

TELEVISION IN
AND AS NEW MEDIA

This is just like television, only you can see
much further.
—Chance, *Being There* (Ashby, 1979)

The effects of technology do not occur at the
level of opinions or concepts, but alter sense
ratios or patterns of perception steadily and
without any resistance.
—Marshall McLuhan, *Understanding Media*

I WALK DOWN THE STREET, safely encapsulated
in my media player's sound bubble. A dog runs past, chased
by its owners, causing chaos on the sidewalk. For a moment I
wish I could pause, back up, rewind, replay the scene, as I
would if it happened on my television or computer screen.
Yet this is not a fully mediated, simulated scene, this is just
everyday life in a thoroughly visually and technologically
mediated culture. I go home and look up videos of dogs on the
Internet, remaking the incident in my imagination. My looking
is shaped by my relationship with and access to information
and to vast numbers of images online and onscreen. And
although I regularly use these present-day technologies such as
music players and computers, I also intuitively utilize television

as a kind of cognitive and cultural map for understanding, ordering, and using the information and images I encounter each day. As a key consumer technology, set into domestic and public environments, television establishes our expectations about media and technology, and it is through television that many people have learned how to be media users and individuals.

Art critic and designer Jessica Helfand observed such a connection between television and new media in her 2001 book *Screen: Essays on Graphic Design, New Media, and Visual Culture*, in which she dedicates an entire chapter to how "Television Did It First: Ten Myths about 'New' Media," noting the irony that "television is rarely—if ever—cited" (9). Even when using technologies as distinct and separate from television as a music/media player or a computer connected to the Internet, my use of those technologies is still informed by my familiarity with, relationship to, and use of television, as I discussed in the introduction.

In this chapter, I explore instances of technological and cultural convergence between TV's old and computer's new media, as seen in hardware, accessories, and devices that allow for televisual functions to be part of using the computer or, in some cases, make the TV itself into a Web and media browser of sorts. To understand these technologies, one must first untangle how the current situation, in which television's influence is so broad, came to be. This has happened even as television's share of the media marketplace is being given up to and combined with other forms and systems that deliver content to consumers (or rather, deliver consumers to advertisers, as has largely been the agenda of American commercial television since the 1940s). First, we examine some of the discourses surrounding both new media—here that term refers primarily to the Internet and its technologies—and the seemingly "old" media of television. In doing so, we must reexamine prior preconceptions about television programming and devices that are often conflated with the medium itself.

Concepts such as televisual style, liveness, temporality, spatiality, as well as TV technologies such as remote controls and digital video recorders and industrial attempts to bridge the gap between TV and new media, all create possible points of convergence between (old and new) media via the (TV) tube or its symbolic use as a referent.[1] "Television" connotes much more than its original literal meaning of sight at a distance. Today, television's channels, networks, tubes, program guides, and more are all part of a media logic used both by those who make and distribute old and new media and those who use it. In a way then, the discourses surrounding television are a *shared language* spoken by media users, and in this chapter I tease out what meanings are embedded in that language.[2]

Reconnecting the Set and the PC

Once referring to the actual cathode ray tube technology used in both early mainframe computing and inside television receivers (sets), the word "tube" is now also a metaphor for video technology and for communication conduits, as can be seen in places ranging from the name of online video portal YouTube to the comments of former Senator Ted Stevens, who infamously referred to the Internet as a "series of tubes"—calling to mind an imaginary version of the Internet as a fiberoptic mess of tubes and wires.[3] As we see, here tubes are being deployed as metaphors for imagining ways to use the Internet (to "broadcast" one's self through the distribution of video footage online via YouTube, a site with the motto "Broadcast Yourself"), or as the actual "stuff" that comprises the Internet's networks. So how, exactly, have television and computer technologies been understood as linked together? How do these instances of "convergence" work? How has television been literally and figuratively linked to computers and computer networks? In this chapter I discuss conjunctions of computers with television, as well as the logics of convergence that surround them. Along with this discussion of aligned technologies, media archaeology is presented as a counterdiscourse to convergence studies, one that pays attention to medium specificity and the history of technology. To that end, qualities and terms often associated with the TV—from networks to tubes to guides—are worth reexamining as evidence for when and how TV invents and coalesces with new media—and when its model is no longer the best way to approach the new.

From the early 1990s on through the present day, the TV-as-computer/computer-as-TV strategy was taken up by leading computer manufacturers and software development firms. Earlier, as chapter 1 discussed, television receivers were utilized as the "natural" monitor component for early computers and computer gaming systems. Contemporary personal computers can, if outfitted with the proper video card, also process and display television. There is a wide range of ancillary computer-television accessories that allow one to "beam" content between devices or utilize a computer as a television set or vice versa. Apple Computer even released the unsuccessful Macintosh TV in 1993—a black case computer equipped with a fourteen-inch Sony Trinitron CRT monitor and a built-in television tuner card and remote (see figure 14). Apple pulled this poorly selling device (the 1993 retail price was over $2,000) from the market only five months after it was released, guaranteeing its place in history as a collector's item.[4] The start-up company WebTV made another early attempt to synergize connections between television and computers in its WebTV "set-top box" as a computer/interactive Web browser accessed via a television receiver. Like the Apple project, WebTV met with very limited commercial success upon its debut in 1995. However, Microsoft saw potential in the marketplace for a home Web browser and multimedia system accessed via the television, and purchased WebTV in 1997, retooling the original technology and releasing updated versions as MSNTV and MSNTV2.

More recently, Elgato Systems and Apple Computer have attempted to situate the personal computer as a site for television viewing, recording, storage, and personalized customer use of televisual content. The German company Elgato has designed and manufactured television tuners and digital video recorders that attach to Apple computers as peripheral devices under the EyeTV brand since 2002.[5] Apple's own "Apple TV" device, launched in January of 2007, is designed to act like a wireless home theater receiver that allows users to "beam" content from their computers to their

14. Macintosh TV computer system, 1993.

television sets (see figure 15). Ironically, the Apple TV device makes useful another Apple "TV"-style component that is standard with most contemporary Macintosh computers—the Mac Remote. Personally I have not found much use for this remote control, as I am typically sitting immediately in front of the computer while using it and do not need to use a remote while "watching" my computer. But the very existence of the Mac Remote indicates Apple's investment in promoting their technology as both personal computer and personal media screen, encouraging a logic of convergence. Although Apple's early 1990s endeavor to make television and computers converge failed, the company now clearly sees that such convergence is finally at hand, and they are ready to be the platform, or better yet, the brand of platforms, on which it takes place.

In 2010 there are music/media players and wireless phones, such as the iPod and iPhone, that have video cameras and video display screens as standard elements, and iPhone applications or "apps" that borrow from television rhetoric, as well as applications that turn either the iPod Touch or iPhone into a remote control device for use with Apple TV and certain software programs. Apple's line of hardware and software programs that invoke connections to television enable a "televisual" mode for users of these devices, all the while redefining the "televisual" itself as newly mobile and miniature via the iPod and iPhone, as well as packaging finite television episodes and software programs to be downloaded from iTunes and viewed on demand via the Apple TV server.

15. Original publicity image from the launch of Apple TV, in which the server hardware is surrounded by a vast plentitude of television imagery.

Apple is not alone in its efforts to bring television to computers. Computer users themselves have a long history of recirculating television content online—through Internet-distributed illegal copies of broadcasts and fan-transcribed scripts. In doing so, these computer users have long watched television's content on computers, as well as utilized television tuner cards that allow PC users to modify their computers into television receivers, much as the Elgato device does for Mac users. And while devices like Apple TV or Web TV allow one to "beam" content from the Internet onto television receivers, these TV/computer "crossovers" indicate both the mobility of content (from TV to the Internet and back again) and illuminate the determination of users (and hardware manufacturers) to make it possible for one technology to function like another.

Meanwhile, Hulu, a joint venture among multinational media conglomerates NBC Universal, News Corporation (Fox), and Providence Equity Partners creates TV/computer/Internet synergy by letting users access old and new television content via high-quality streaming media run through their World Wide Web browser software. Here the software and its protocols—reminding us again of the crucial role played by network protocols—is vital to media convergence, while media content itself is part of a larger database of on-call, on-demand information. Hulu succeeds by recycling old content alongside new, utilizing the preexisting infrastructure and technologies of streaming media and networks and the discourse of television, now envisioned in their 2008–2009 advertisements as an immediate way for Hulu, represented in the ads as an "alien" corporation, to "suck the brains" of vast wasteland viewers and destroy the world. The advertisements star famous television personalities—Alec Baldwin, Seth MacFarlane, Eliza Dushku—as shills for a corporate synergy plan that is presented as both science fiction fun and a mockery of the wasteland discourse of media consumers as "cultural dopes," a term taken from the cultural studies debates around how to best study the activities of and speak to mass media audiences and consumers.[6] Here convergence is a fun new way to use both TV and one's computer, all the while producing more trackable data for Hulu providers to analyze and develop marketing strategies for smart, computer savvy audiences ready to have their brains sucked out.

Clearly television's relationship to new media occurs on multiple fronts—through discourse and reference to television's presentational styles and genres, through hardware and software that literally link television and computers, and through industry practices and approaches that imagine the Internet and television as linked discursive spaces where stories can be told and audiences found. In examining television and computers alongside one another, I can better understand how the received knowledge surrounding TV has been translated to the digital cultures and objects that so often borrow from and refer back to this pervasive medium.

WATCHING, NOT USING, MEDIA

Here's a true confession, an actual one, not the kind you would find on a reality show with a special "confessional" room set aside for dramaturgy: *Sometimes I just want to sit back and watch.* Yet computers, Blackberries, TiVo, push-to-talk phones, gaming systems, iPods—all require me to interact *both* physically and mentally with the content I encounter. This push-me-pull-you quality of media, as described by Henry Jenkins and others, is the crux of the contemporary cultural problem that television and its messy boundaries present (Jenkins, McPherson, and Shattuc 5). Yet, there is also a kind of flexibility in media that allows for both the push and the pull of interactivity that happens in between more passive moments of viewing. Elsewhere I have described this as a kind of passivity that is shot through with interactivity, with the potential to engage and use media in newfound ways.[7]

Televisual styles and structures inform the visualities of new media: network infrastructures, video images, editing styles, the seriality of TV episodes and modes of accessing them (channel surfing, multitasking, timeshifting) are all key elements of and metaphors for new media forms and cultures.[8] Although, as discussed in the introduction, new media and cinema are often compared—through attempts for "total cinema" by virtual reality technologies or in industrial comparisons between early cinema and "early" new media forms—television's role in and influence upon new media continue to be undertheorized and overlooked. We must, however, look to television and how this medium both subtly and unsubtly has shaped our expectations and experiences of computer and new media.

BLACK BOX FALLACIES AND BOXES OF WIRES

In his book *Convergence Culture*, Henry Jenkins persuasively argues against overly simplistic theories of media convergence—those premised on a "black box fallacy" that unites separate media functions and forms (14–15). Instead, Jenkins tells us that the key components of convergence are media users themselves and how they synthesize and combine different media into new, emergent forms and tools (2, 24). Although I agree with much of what Jenkins has to say, particularly his critique of naïve and utopian theories of how all media are coming together, I want to briefly resurrect the concept of the black box. Jenkins critiques the way the black box fallacy "reduces media change to technological change and strips aside the cultural levels [of convergence]" (15). Yet figuratively, this notion of a unifying black box of media is useful, particularly since television is arguably a central part of this imagined convergence technology. Even the idea that media is received via a "box" goes back at least as far as television if not back to radio before it.[9] Of course, it is also arguable that Jenkins's "black box" refers to computer, telecommunications, and entertainment technologies beyond broadcast media like radio and television. But as a "black box," television contains all of the components often associated with media convergence: multiple modes of communication/reception, the ability to record and produce one's own media (using ancillary technologies), interactivity, and, increasingly, high-speed connectivity to a communications network. So why can't TV be the black box, or why is such a model flawed? And, if television is not the black box of convergence, what is its role as and in new media?

Perhaps alongside the dream of a singular, unifying black box of media, we should also consider the material reality of points of convergence today, which can be found in what I have long referred to as a "box of wires." My own box of wires is just that—the cardboard box that my first TiVo digital video recorder arrived in, now filled to capacity with a wide range of audio and video cables, adapters, power cords, extra Ethernet cables, digital camera output cables, extension cords, and the like. Inside I have also kept manuals and my own hand-drawn diagrams of how to connect technologies together, sometimes in ways unintended by the manufacturer (my favorite diagram is a complex one showing how to hook two VCR decks to my TiVo and then, of course, how to make the accompanying cable and television receiver connections). While it is certainly possible that I am an oddball, throwing all my miscellaneous and sundry connectors and adapters together into one box, I have a hunch that many computer users and TV viewers today have similar, if not more elaborate, boxes of wires lying around their homes. What can this box of extraneous cables and adapters tell us about how media comes together? Or, more pointedly, about how media does not always converge as promised?

For one thing, the box of wires demonstrates how both knowledge and connectivity are key to the "trans" part of transmedia and convergence: without the ability to connect machines to each other and the Radio Shack parts to do it, there is no way for media to jump from platform to platform. Just as Internet protocols enable the emergence of a worldwide network, cable, video, and audio adapters, along with wireless routers, enable technological convergence to take place. But, perhaps more important, the box of wires shows how reliant media convergence is upon users and their determination to make (intended or unintended) connectivity happen. It also represents all the mundane ways in which both media and convergence fail to happen—the dropped connection or call between a digital video recorder and its mainframe server can leave online schedules and menus blank or planned recordings unrecorded, while incorrect settings can also leave technologies connected but "dumb" and unable to output data.

I often like to joke about the evocative and seamless language William Gibson used when imagining cyberspace in his novel *Neuromancer* (1986). Gibson wrote: "The transition to cyberspace, when he hit the switch, was instantaneous" (55). Outside of science fiction, most users of the Internet, digital television, DVDs, and handheld media players do not get to "instantaneously" transition into the cyberspace of media content, despite a cultural emphasis and value placed upon the speed and ubiquity of connectivity. Instead, one is left with slowly reloaded Web sites, dropped calls, missing content. As a result, we need both the black box of convergence and the box of wires to participate in media convergence cultures. Perhaps those who are fond of promoting the notion that digital technologies have allowed for greater interaction with media—a supposed truism of new media that is often repeated in both the industry as self-promotion and in academia as utopian hopes for technology's (assumed) democratizing power—should look instead at how media users now learn and acquire new knowledge about media technologies while we configure our equipment as much as we do while watching the content it delivers. Sometimes the "materiality" of digital convergences is all too real and not at all an experience of speed or instantaneousness interaction with glossy, high-tech content.

When thinking about how television is central to uses and understanding of new media, one needs to ask: *How is new media not just television all over again?* This is not easy to answer, for if one argues that television is interactive (just less so, or, more precisely, differently so) and hypermediated, combining a multitude of different kinds of content, all the while scrambling public and private space and selves, television starts to sound great deal like new media technologies and computer networks. And certainly, when one gets down to circuit boards, hard drives, and wires, the differences are fairly subtle between television and new media, especially when one considers that television devices and computer devices increasingly have complementary hardware, as discussed in chapter 1. In the current generation of video game consoles, systems like the Playstation 3 and Xbox 360 are designed to be all-in-one gaming and media servers.

Yet, culturally and ideologically, the televisual dispositif carries with it the baggage of mass media and mid-twentieth century culture. While televisual innovators are many, television—despite its critical champions—is persistently and widely (mis)understood as emblematic of couch potato culture, of the era of staged media events and global media messages.[10]

In her recent book, *Control and Freedom: Power and Paranoia in the Age of Fiber Optics* (2006), Wendy Hyui Kyong Chun argues for an approach to the study of computers, networks, and the various media technologies I have been discussing here that she specifically refers to as "new media" rather than digital media or digital culture, software studies or cyberculture (17–18). Chun's approach is informed by two fields—visual culture studies and media archaeology (17). Yet she also wants to critique approaches that privilege either the "computer layer" or "culture layer" in their analyses of new media, to borrow terms from legal scholar Lawrence Lessig.[11] As Chun puts it, "Software cannot be physically separately from hardware, only ideologically" (19). One could make a similar argument about television, a medium whose very apparatus is utterly conflated with its content. Yet television can also be understood through its culture/content and data/computer layers: TV software (programs or content) is only accessible through its hardware (production equipment, satellite and cable relays, cable and television receivers). In this new media era, it is nearly impossible to separate out culture and computer layers that are so deeply interconnected and can only be experienced through the successful activation of both culture and computers together.

In foregrounding her theoretical agenda and attempt to bridge fields when studying what she calls the new "mass media," Chun takes the bull by the horns and wrestles with the ideological gunk embedded in naming the new. Whatever you call it, the question remains: how is this stuff not just the old all over again, in some slightly modified, rehashed format? Or, conversely, if it is just a rehash, does that matter? Chun's choice to apply methodologies from visual culture studies and media archaeology is an intriguing one: both fields prioritize theory and attention to form, while they differ on their understandings of the importance of media specificity.[12] But her methods are also emblematic of a kind of interdisciplinary blindness that has emerged alongside these emergent/new media forms. Scholars trained in disciplines centered on aesthetics, form, and culture see in new media certain stylistic trends and shifting user positions, while those educated in linguistic or philosophical disciplines notice new, more activated textualities and forms of reading. Chun herself, like Lev Manovich, is that rare scholar who can both code and decode—and who teaches the construction of new media alongside its theorization. Yet, perhaps because she is already doing the important business of coding, decoding, and digging into a medium's archaeology, Chun's facility with the tools and history of film and media theory is somewhat lacking.[13] But Chun's approach to new media is a productive model that somewhat sidesteps convergence debates through her visual and archaeological methodology.

Scholarly approaches to television and new media often include social science and humanities methodologies, both of which can benefit from media archaeology, the approach Chun places alongside her visual culture analysis. Through this tactic, one gains historical context and depth, as well as comparisons with historical precedents for the study of new and emerging media. Media archaeology, largely practiced outside of the United States by field leaders such as Siegfried Zielinski, Friedrich Kittler, and Erkki Huhtamo, prioritizes the deep historicity and specificity of media while theorizing how media sound, sense, and imagery have tremendous cultural and personal effects. This approach is attentive to the history of technology and to medium specificity—what properties are unique to each medium—analyzing those elements, for instance, that make television something other than film. Works such as Zielinski's *Audiovision* even historically compare different media technologies such as film, television, and radio with each other throughout their histories. Often these historical accounts are combined with theorizations of a medium's cultural importance and roles, as in Kittler's canonical "Gramophone, Film, Typewriter" essay first published in *October* 41 (1987).

Despite such critical attention to medium specificity, media archaeology methodology does not prioritize the aesthetic and formal elements of particular works or objects in media history and in media representations the way that the fields of film and media studies typically do. Even scholars in television and cultural studies who do try to bring the medium into the new media discussion do so in ways that, perhaps inadvertently, tame television's cultural centrality and effects. In her short essay "Television's Next Season?" Lynn Spigel considers the future of television studies and, in doing so, discusses the impact of digital media studies and visual culture studies on the field. She cannily points out how, "Often, it seems the term 'new media' works to reinvest television in yet another set of cultural hierarchies, because the term suggests something avant-garde, high-tech, revolutionary, utopian, and fundamentally 'other' than ordinary TV" (84).[14] Clearly, with the tendency of some scholars to continually compare new media with cinema and the apparent cultural biases to see the new as somehow both other and, perhaps, more than TV, there is much at stake in understanding just how television is implicated in and connected to the emergence of that which goes under the name "new media."

How, then, is it possible to both isolate the formal qualities that mark certain media as "televisual" and keep in mind the constant comparisons with other media—both old and new—that those elements call to mind? As Amanda Lotz has noted, "We must now think about television as a highly diversified medium; even as 'watching television' has continued to signify a set of widely recognizable behaviors, the singularity and coherence of their experience has come to be fleeting" (80). Just as "television" is an abstract and shifting technology and public medium, the devices we use to access it, as well as the settings in which we encounter television also continue to proliferate and change, despite the rhetoric of technological convergence surrounding TV and linking it to other media.

Although there are television studies texts that go into much greater detail on the relationship between television and its formal aesthetic qualities, the conflation of television broadcast with liveness, televisual space, and the ways in which time unfolds on TV, I want to briefly put those issues into relief here. The discourses surrounding televisual form, simultaneity or liveness, space, and time prefigure and in fact make way for the debates surrounding new media. At the same time, public debates and discussions around television are also part and parcel of new media discourse, for television is not simply a precursor to the new but is continually caught up in those forms and technologies labeled, marketed, and branded as new. Or, as Spigel puts it, "Insofar as television studies has been centrally concerned with similar issues, and insofar as television now converges with digital platforms, it seems only right that people who study television would also study the Internet and other digital devices" ("Television's Next Season" 84).

TELEVISION AND FORM

In order to trace out the connections between television and new media, it is necessary to understand the aspects of television (both the technology and the cultural form) that mark it as "new media," such as its screen, its technological structure, its liveness, and, for lack of a better word, its ambiance. One key difference between television and cinema relevant to new media is the form of image display entailed by each. Whereas films are projected onto a large screen, television images are relayed and scanned onto an electronic display/monitor and broadcast over the airwaves or received via cable and satellite technologies. During the middle part of the twentieth century, spectators and consumers began to encounter new kinds of screened entertainments—from television and drive-in theaters to images of new mainframe computers that were operated from terminal "windows" with screens reliant on the same cathode ray tube technology as television.[15] Through the popular press and television news reports, the public could follow the emergence of the massive, mainframe computers used at military research institutions and major research universities.[16]

Unlike cinema, where the spectator is immobilized in a fixed position, gaze focused upon the oversized screen, television spectators, or viewers as they are more commonly called, have traditionally looked at a significantly smaller image and are free to move about while the television is on.[17] In fact, some theorists have argued that television is not necessarily a medium but should instead be considered a "mode" or a "cultural flow," as Raymond Williams suggested, since it is "always on" and accessible by the viewing public and does not have a closed or fixed narrative format.[18] Instead, television programming is structured by repetitions and representational strategies that have imitated commercially successful styles, genres, and formats. In fact, television's "flow" has been formative to the field of television studies, as have the attendant characteristics associated with it. Critical issues such as televisual style, liveness, space, and time are all deserving of much greater attention than I am able to give them here. Instead, I hope to illuminate how these key ways of framing or understanding television have also been caught up in the technological and cultural understanding of television as live, popular, banal, media flows. This framing of television also has a predictive aspect to it, as it enables the recognition of new media as interactive, imperceptibly fast, computer technologies that do not necessarily replicate television's form but instead become a new, virtual location for encounters with televisual content and style.

THE TEMPORALITY OF LIVENESS, ACCESSED ON DEMAND

As a temporally transmitted medium, television enabled a new period of mediated instantaneity with the live transmission of broadcast images. As Jane Feuer and numerous other television scholars have theorized, the category of "liveness" became central to television's media specificity, singling out television as a spontaneous and unscripted medium when compared with the fixed, "canned" narratives of cinema.[19] Television's distinct status as an electronic medium continues to be demonstrated today in the development of new televisual technologies such as digital video recorders, which link the experience of viewing television with the experiences of computer culture and the hypermediated structures of the World Wide Web. In fact, William Boddy claims that liveness or televisual simultaneity, alongside domesticity and a nationalist television discourse, is one of the aspects of

American television most threatened by digital video recorders and other asynchronous new media devices that decrease the medium's mass audience (*New Media* 103–104).

Televisual "liveness" is a quality often conflated with and collapsed upon the medium itself and is produced through structures that cue the viewer to the "live" recording or broadcast of programming, such as "live from . . ." graphics, split screens of reporters in different locales, the unplanned or unanticipated image or sound (such as Janet Jackson's 2004 Super Bowl "wardrobe malfunction," which cost CBS a $550,000 fine from the Federal Communications Commission), and the "back to the studio or anchor desk" structure of television news. While news programming connotes its liveness on a regular basis, other television programming also works to appear live—either through documentary structures or by being recorded in front of a live studio audience. Like the other media discussed in this book, liveness implies that images are unscripted, unrehearsed, and less "fixed" than images that do not connote or promote their "this-is-going-on-ness" (Doane 222). For early television viewers, the liveness of *all* television programming was an added attraction and one that was distinct from cinematic spectatorship, in which the same narratives unfolded every time a film was shown. On the Internet, liveness is also a valued quality, often connoting truth, realism, or even the "authenticity" of amateur video productions filled with "dead air" or awkward gaps that lack narrative progression and action.

One can see Internet technologies like webcams or, more recently, YouTube clips and live, streamed Web media providing online audiences and users with an experience not unlike that of live television broadcast viewers, especially when those same images are also banal and produced or viewed remotely from where the images were produced. Indeed, many former "mass" spectacles like presidential inaugurations or state funerals can be watched more easily online in workplaces that support broadband but lack broadcast. Much of watching a video blog or "vlog" post on YouTube—or watching any user-produced images (as opposed to images that users have distributed online but not made)—is about waiting for the unpredictable to happen, waiting to "get" what makes that video distinctive. In this way then, sites like YouTube aggregate liveness for us, let us asynchronously "be there" in the moment.

EVERYDAY SPACES

The televisual medium, whether broadcast or satellite-relayed, is an amazingly flexible and pervasive presence in everyday life. Anna McCarthy aptly describes this aspect of television as an "ambient" component of public spaces and visualities: "TV integrates into everyday environments so well that we barely notice its presence in 'our taverns and our metropolitan streets'—and to update Walter Benjamin's famous litany, our shopping malls, delis, Laundromats, airports, and other places besides" (2–3). McCarthy's arguments about public installations of television sets are echoed in other television scholarship, such as Mary Ann Watson's claim that "watching the TV set at the corner bar was the way many Americans became acquainted with the new medium" (9). In contemporary American culture, television is so widespread that its presence is barely noticeable—it is ambient, unassuming, "white noise" in the background of daily life.[20] In many ways, new media technologies have been modeled on television's ubiquitous, unassuming place in the media landscape. As J. David Bolter and Richard Grusin wrote, one of the key aims of new media is to be *immediate*: to blend into the environment as a ubiquitous and ever-present part of the everyday (21–31). And iPods, laptops, smart media, and wireless phones have succeeded at this task; indeed we are more likely to notice their *absence* rather than their presence in our daily routines.[21]

TIME AND TELEVISION

Temporally, television has also changed the everyday experience and perception of actual time through its schedule.[22] An early television text, Thomas Hutchinson's *Here Is Television, Your Window to the World*, published in 1946, promised that television would play an important role in the future of both telecommunications and global politics, its "window" creating a new context for communication and understanding: "In television we have an instrument that can make possible our identification with our fellow men over the face of the earth. We shall hear them speak to us and see them clearly in their appeal for understanding. They will see and hear us, and we must make them know our purposes. This has been possible through the newsreel, but television will make the immediacy of relationship beyond escape" (vi).

Later, in *Here Is Television*, Hutchinson again returns to the importance of television's immediacy, claiming that "the really vital thing is that by means of television, either in the home or in the theater, everyone in America will be able some day to see everything that happens anywhere in this world we live in" (321). Like telegraphy and radio before it, and the Internet after, the new technology of television was seen early on as a solution to social problems and as a means for an expansive and newly "global" reality (Sconce, *Haunted Media* 11). And while early television did bring about changes, it did not necessarily resolve social problems—in fact, throughout its history television has been blamed for myriad social problems—most notably the moral panics around issues of television and youth.[23]

Another TV structure that Internet and new media rework is that of the rerun—the re-presentation of material originally broadcast and now shown again (to either new or repeat audiences). The disjunctive and uneven experience of new media—in which one's individual path through content is highly subjective and varied (one person's new media experience might well be another's old *new media* experience) means that most online media is always, perpetually being rerun and returned to and even duplicated and "backed up" as files on a server. This is quite different from television's rerun.

The rerun has been an important formal category of television's so-called "essence," as Jenny Nelson argues in her essay, "The Dislocation of Time: A Phenomenology of Television Reruns." Nelson argues that reruns are key to television structure and its phenomenological "internationality" (80). Rerun television programs are compelling for their very lack of narrative suspense—the audience already knows the outcome. Yet in their familiarity and immediate, seeming proximity to our everyday lives, television reruns are the "comfort food" that viewers consistently turn back to, again and again. Nelson calls this the "rerun as rerun" aspect of television, claiming: "Television experience works according to a *fort/da* dialectic—a *telos*—of endless presence and absence and substitution, based as much on non-narrativized displeasure as pleasure, in which each moment rewrites the other" (88, 91). Using Freud's discussion of the fort/da (literally "gone" and "there" in German) in which an adult plays with an infant by repeatedly making objects appear and disappear, therefore introducing the child to the concepts of absence, presence, reappearance and repetition, Nelson claims that the viewer of rerun programming derives much of his or her pleasure from their engagement with that which they have already seen. Nelson's essay attempts to apply phenomenology and critical theory to the discourse of television studies in order to describe how the regular practice of watching TV and encountering syndicated or rerun programming is a defining characteristic of the medium.

In Nelson's view, the rerun is a central part of the television experience, a repetitive "essence" of the televisual that is not about Raymond Williams's notion of "flow" nor about a textually defined viewer experience, since the viewer does not engage with the text as narrative. Flow, as theorized by Williams, describes the open-endedness of the televisual and the way that programs and commercials seamlessly flow together to create the category of experience known as the televisual (89–91). Instead, as Nelson theorizes, the rerun is (though she does not use this term) "ambient" programming—just filling up space and time for unfocused viewers.

Digital, new media time is also programmable and experienced differently through the application of nonlinear editing and the ability of digitally recorded images to be easily reordered and accessed at will. This leads to such phenomena as the instant replay, which Chris Hanson has noted, "erodes the [televisual] medium's conceptual (albeit somewhat contentious) pillars of 'flow' and 'liveness' to a significant degree by way of its interruptive and erstwhile nature" (51).

Controlling the Remote:
Opening Up the Black Box

Television is also a technology that can, for ambitious and technologically inclined viewers, be an "open-box" experience. One can remove the plastic casing that holds the TV and adjust the inner workings of the television set to fix picture quality or other aspects of TV reception.[24]

TV viewers gain a sense of immediate control over television technology since they can select from a set schedule of programs to view and change those selections as desired. Their level of interactivity is therefore higher than the level of interactivity of cinema spectators, who must watch fixed narratives at specific times (though film spectators select which narrative to watch, just as TV viewers do). The television schedule, structured to match the daily routines of life (meal times, leisure time), allows the TV viewer an illusion of great control and choice, as do remote controls and other ancillary TV technologies (Browne 71). Nick Browne's seminal 1986 essay on the television schedule establishes how the logic of American television is grounded in its presentational schedule and the demarcation and categorization of programming according to a twenty-four-hour clock, with "daytime television" and "primetime television" as two distinct and fundamental semiotic categories for programming. But what happens when that schedule becomes an electronic hypertext that television viewers can navigate, sort, reorder, and access upon demand while watching television, instead of a schedule that is a relatively fixed and stable document published in the daily newspaper and weekly *TV Guide* magazine? This, quite literally, is media convergence: computer software applied, delivered, and utilized via the television set.[25]

Significantly, television networks and advertisers are also currently working to develop legislation against this particular technology of interaction because it allows viewers to "skip" commercials, undermining the industry's economic base (Bowman).[26] With the new conveniences and appealing styles of "digital" television culture—high-definition programming and a new generation of redesigned television receivers, cable systems that deliver televisual content along with high-speed Internet access, interactivity, and customization of programming via the "smart" set and its accoutrements, comes a new set of problems—depending upon whom you talk to. Television industries must rework their models of advertising and sponsorship to adapt to consumer changes, and new industries—such as the digital video recorder industry—must find a way to market new technological capabilities to consumers (who skip commercials) while appeasing the content producers and advertisers (who use the TiVo Program Guide software to deliver specialized, targeting advertising to those consumers who are now "skipping" traditional spot ads). Television scholar William Boddy discusses these shifts in the televisual in far greater detail in his book *New Media and Popular Imagination: Launching Radio, Television and Digital Media in the United States* (2004). As Boddy puts it, "Not withstanding the manifest turmoil within the US television industry at the beginning of the twenty-first century, it is easy to be skeptical of the self-interested claims for technologically driven fundamental change in the medium, especially in light of decades of unsuccessful business ventures advanced under the banners of technological convergence and viewer interactivity" (136).

Or, to put it another way: competing discourses of change, convergence, and interactivity are an integral part of American television and its shift toward the digital. We have good reason to question how and why such changes in the medium are taking place in this particular historical moment. "Innovation" does not happen in a vacuum, nor does the drive to provide "better" television, which, in the current technological climate often connotes more interactive, higher resolution and definition of screen images and, of course, choice in one's TV.

Historically, television sets have always required owner/user "interaction." Changes in weather might cause reception to be spotty, and television antennas regularly required some kind of "tweak" or service. In the late 1970s and early 1980s, the introduction of pay cable television services brought new hardware components like set-top boxes and indoor/outdoor cable wires into the homes of millions of television viewers. Today, as discussed earlier in this chapter, a television set can be "configured" as one of many components in a home theater system, including digital surround sound, digital video disc (DVD) players, video cassette recorders, digital video recorders, personal computers, and other electronic devices. Additionally, this media hardware might also record and play multiple analog and digital data compression formats—such as DVD players that also play Blu-ray DVD, MP3, and CD files. Digital video recorders present the illusion of greater control and choice over television programming, since programs can be time-compressed and edited through the viewer's use of the technology, yet this is fundamentally choice within a closed system. One cannot make new programming using a TiVo (though, hypothetically, a TiVo connected to a VCR could do crude montage editing), one can only sort and deploy preprogrammed options offered up by television networks. Yet although consumers do not have the capability to make their own media, digital video recorders point toward the convergence of analog content with digital display and storage formats, as well as the cross-pollination of media style and content between different platforms such as television and the Internet.[27]

Such technological intermingling—of devices once categorized either as televisual and entertainment-oriented or as relegated to the business worlds of computing (spreadsheets, databases, etc.)—attests to how, in both promoted, possible uses and actual user practices, televisual consumption is now increasingly linked to practical, economically oriented processes and the use of software by consumers and viewers through either their remote controls or the device that is accessed in conjunction with television viewing—the computer. Such connections, passed on to consumers as "upgrades" to their cable television service or encountered as one struggles to operate an increasingly complex remote control, are easy to miss. Hence the epigraph from Marshall McLuhan that opens this chapter. The true power of technologies to shift cultural paradigms are often the things we overlook, the way our "patterns of perception" are altered so that, for example, the strange new remote control becomes a familiar tool, does indeed happen unremarkably and routinely, just as McLuhan claimed they would. Tubes, networks, channels, boxes—terms once applied primarily to television—are more than simple metaphors. They provide a model for thinking about both old and new media together—and they set our expectations for approaching new media through the application of these inherited terms. The Internet is far more than a series of tubes, and if we approach it as such, we limit what it can be. Perhaps this is a tenuous point where new media and old media best diverge rather than converge? And yet, one often finds new media emerging out of the old, as the next chapter will demonstrate.

In chapter 4, I analyze remote control devices, game controllers, and video game systems that address the user through visceral and embodied experiences, seeing how one potential endpoint of media convergence—the user—is configured alongside the interactive technologies he or she encounters. In doing so, one can understand how these earlier instances connecting television sets to game consoles imagined the space of gaming in relation to how contemporary systems, like Nintendo's Wii and the industrywide use of "rumbleshock" technologies envelop us within their ludic space and experience. Here are new uses for television that rely upon the earlier moments of convergence between video game systems, computers, and TV in the 1970s, as discussed in chapter 1.

This approach to video games as embodied encounters with television explicitly complicates received ideas about "television programming" and "interactivity" through an investigation of video game systems designed to make television do and be more than just a screening platform for content produced by television networks. Instead, video games are pieces of computer software meant to be played via the television set. This model of interactive television upsets one's expectations about passive versus active viewership, as video games entail interactive, embodied participation in order for the software to run. Yet, quite often, video games are not looked to as a model for interactive television programming but are instead understood as an industry separate from and in some ways in opposition to the television sets that the games are played upon, and through and the domestic spaces that gamers and viewers play in, on, and "leave behind."

CHAPTER 4

ALT-CTRL

THE FREEDOM OF REMOTES AND CONTROLS

I'm sitting around . . . *thinking about what*
you can do with a TV set other than tuning
in channels you don't want. And I came up
with the concept of doing games, building
something for $19.95. This was 1966, in
August.

—Ralph Baer, inventor of the Magnavox
Odyssey television console gaming system
(quoted in Kent, *The Ultimate History of*
Video Games, emphasis added)

Hey, tell me the truth . . . are we still in
the game?

—*eXistenZ* (Cronenberg, 1999)

THAT VIDEO GAMES AND THOSE ITEMS under-
stood to fit within the video game "phylum" of media—video
console platforms, computer games, flash media and other "down
time" games, handheld games, games embedded in time pieces or
incorporated into other technologies as secondary elements—are
a major industry and force in electronic entertainments today
is undeniable.[1] But situating video games in relation to television and as an element of television is a less expected claim. In
today's entertainment marketplace, video and computer gamers
are the eager consumers who are largely responsible for the

rapid growth of the 21.33-billion-dollar gaming industry.[2] It is crucial to think about gaming beyond its role as digital entertainment. Video games expand our understanding of how we use the medium of television, and in so doing, games force us to rethink the field of television studies itself. In fact, some games researchers have argued that the modality of gaming will become increasingly dominant as a way to solve problems collectively in the future. Game scholar and futurist Jane McGonigal has lectured widely about how games can be applied to nongame "real world" problems. As she puts it, "Games give you new models for looking at the world."[3] Yet games are largely misunderstood within the broader realm of popular culture, perhaps due to generational and other cultural divides. It may be that the biggest way in which games are misrecognized by those who don't play is the widespread notion that playing a video game is a form of pure release, play, and enjoyment. As Steven Johnson wrote in *Everything Bad Is Good for You: How Today's Popular Culture Is Actually Making Us Smarter*, "The dirty little secret of gaming is how much time you spend not having fun. You may be frustrated; you may be confused or disoriented; you may be stuck. . . . If this is mindless escapism, it's a strangely masochistic version" (25–26).

Games then, are more than escapism, more than entertainment, and they are possibly a model for how to look at and approach the world around us. Seen in conjunction with another device one uses to "play" the TV set, the remote control, the dynamics of user agency, interactivity, and "control" over the television emerge as key ways that television sets, remotes, and controllers all provide new, "alternative" modes of using TV.

Another important yet mistaken scrap of widely received knowledge about playing video and other screen-based games is that, through interactive elements and narrative devices, games somehow become dangerously transparent and immediate for those who play them, in turn enabling a gamer to "tune in" to a game while "tuning out" of material reality. In this chapter I explore both the thinking behind such claims and the actual technologies of video gaming in order to disconnect these powerful and deeply entrenched beliefs about gamers and the subject/

object relations they encounter when they play. I also reconnect games to television as both a (primarily) domestic object and as an object of academic study. If this were a longer book solely on video games and gaming, there are other parts of these questions I would consider; in particular, I would look more closely at who plays games and how those gamer audiences are imagined in the popular press. Luckily, the burgeoning field of video game scholarship does just that in places as diverse as the online journal *Game Studies* and in books like the anthology *Second Person: Role-Playing and Stories in Games and Playable Media* (Wardrip-Fruin and Harrigan 2007) and Celia Pearce's *Communities of Play: Emergent Cultures in Multiplayer Games and Virtual Worlds* (2009).

What do video games and how one uses them have to do with television and its invention of new media? Such games make new, innovative uses out of television sets and video monitors, turning the television set into another type of media device, as discussed in chapter 1. Although it is often assumed or taken for granted that a television set is made for receiving television programming, engineers like Ralph Baer and other electronics tinkerers saw the potential for television to serve as a key component for home gaming systems. Likewise, in 1958 Willy Higinbotham utilized a device dependent on the same display technology as television—the oscilloscope—in his laboratory at Brookhaven National Laboratory when he created what is often cited as the original video game, *Tennis for Two*. Through the visual display of a television set, video games are a technology that links computing to the leisure activities of TV and extend what "television" is in the process—as the quote from video game inventor Ralph Baer at the start of this chapter suggests. This chapter uncovers what the interactive modalities of video game system input devices and systems reliant upon human physical interactivity as a primary mode of interaction can reveal about the future of both television and new media as entwined technological objects.

Hardware: Game Controls

Since the launch of the Atari video computer system in 1976, video games have been a key way of using television sets as something other than program receivers, and video game systems have functioned as an alternate model of televisual space, mapping onto the TV screen a multitude of immersive game worlds and environments. By examining the input devices used to interact with video game systems, one can see how gamer identity and identification are constructed in relationship to virtual video game spaces, which in turn are a specific manifestation of televisual space that is now understood as a deeply interactive and embodied media zone. While video games potentially draw gamers into the screen space of the game through interactive storytelling devices and game play, they clearly also significantly extend televisual space beyond the TV screen through "force feedback" technologies on handheld game controllers that allow gamers to actually feel the rumble, shock, and action of the game as corporeal sensations linked to on-screen game play. Instead of just drawing gamers into the virtual worlds represented, onscreen contemporary video games also extend the space of the game out into the space traditionally reserved for televisual spectatorship and consumption.[4] In doing so, contemporary video game systems mark that space out as one of action and engagement, rather than the inaction and passive reception that is stereotypically associated with television viewing. Gamers, especially those who play on contemporary systems with body-sensing controls, are markedly not couch potatoes, the stereotype that is all too often applied to TV viewers. In this way then, video gaming, through its cognitive and physical interactivity, presents a counter-narrative about the television experience as an active, physically and cognitively engaged pursuit.[5]

Throughout much of the early academic discourse surrounding new media culture, the cyberpunk desire to escape or transcend mundane reality—as demonstrated in countless science fiction novels, films, and television programs—is often discussed as symptomatic of a desire to leave the "meat" of the body behind in exchange for a perfect virtual body accessed through a screen or virtual reality interface/input device. Playing a video game is a relatively risk-free and socially acceptable way of engaging in a bit of virtual body play—one gets to repeatedly "do over" an action or relive an experience indefinitely until one has perfected the necessary game skill to advance through the game. This play with the virtual body through fictive game worlds is also a play with identity. When I game I am both player and character simultaneously—in the virtual space of the game I am both the game character Mario and Sheila Murphy, the player. If my avatar were simply a narrative element of the game like a character, he would effortlessly complete every level of the game. But since my avatar is imbued with both the in-game artificial intelligence that gives him some of Mario's style and skill and my gamer ability to control and manage the virtual Mario, he stumbles and fails repeatedly. My "meat-body" has tainted his virtual-body, for together we constitute the player-character. Like a 1990s cyberpunk in mirror shades, I haven't left reality behind after all, just viewed it through a particular lens.

What, then, of this new digital, virtual identity discovered via video games? How can I reconcile it with a discourse of digital media identity and media identification? The topic of identity has been much explored within new media studies— though the result has been a series of prognosticating and often celebratory essays around identity-in-flux or free-play. In his introduction to the anthology *Web. Studies: Rewiring Media Studies for the Digital Age* (2000), British media theorist David Gauntlett bemoans the "tedious and repetitive" academic attention paid to the concept of online identity-play that has manifested itself in numerous scholarly articles on cyberculture, which, according to Gauntlett, "basically all say 'cyberspace . . . you can play with identity . . . nobody knows who you really are . . . gosh . . . ' but fail to develop any theoretical insights beyond this once-engaging thought" (15). Much of the early critical writing on identity in digital media studies foregrounded questions of gender and performance, and the proliferation of virtual identities in cyberspace. During the 1990s, academic discussions of virtual and digital technologies, spaces, and identities often triumphed the virtual as a realm where one could escape "lived" reality and act "freely" in the realm of the "technological sublime"—in a cyberspace that was untainted by the social realities and inequalities of class, race, and gender (among others).[6]

Sociologist Sherry Turkle describes the video game variation on this theme in her book *Life on the Screen* (1995). Turkle writes that, for some players, "with practice the rules became semiautomatic, and successful playing required entering a state in which you left the real world behind" (67). This emphasis on the phantasmal aspects of virtual identity is also an emphasis on interactivity and agency, unlike the passive consumption that was thought to characterize mass entertainment (read: television or cinema). The rhetoric surrounding video game systems often echoes this celebration of interactivity and agency, which also foregrounds active, individual choices and the ability to control virtual environments. Clearly these are powerful concepts for a variety of new media forms.

Perhaps the quickest way to cut through the tangled relationships between body, identity, virtuality, and agency is to interrogate notions of interactivity in the domains of both gaming and more traditional forms of television viewing. Since its diffusion into American culture as a conveyer of broadcast programming, television has required its viewers to interact with their receivers or sets—first through direct physical contact with the set's channel and picture controls and its antenna, and later through remote control devices, as well as cable adapters/receivers, video cassette recorders, and their respective remote controls, too. Eventually, digital technologies became available to consumers that performed many of the original "interactions" with the television, albeit now facilitated by new hardware and software. Digital video recorders, often contained as part of a digital cable package, facilitate recording and timeshifting programs while digital video disc players, including Blu-ray players that may allow networked access to services like Netflix on Demand, allow one to interact with the television set as a screen for filmic content rather than as a broadcast device.

On the other hand, video game systems are designed for interactivity and have always relied upon specific, customized remote control devices that are designed for facilitating game play. Using trackballs, joysticks, and a wide array of buttons, among other inputs, these devices also remotely control the on-screen content that the television displays. Although traditional computers still depend upon some variation of the keyboard and mouse setup for user input, video game systems have never had industrywide standardized game controllers, and often third-party manufacturers produce custom controllers like automobile and airplane steering devices or other alternatives to sanctioned, official system hardware.

What both remote controls and game controllers demonstrate is how deeply physical one's interaction with the television can be. A remote or controller becomes a second-nature component in the hand of the experienced user, who operates it by rote and relies upon so-called "muscle-memory" to navigate a program guide screen or engage with virtual foes in a game.[7] Remote controls and game controllers, despite their capacity to become unremarked upon and seemingly automatic "extensions" of the gamer/viewer/user, are crucial, tactile points of contact between the media consumer and his or her on-screen, digital proxy, even if that proxy is as mundane as a highlighted time-slot in Program Guide software. These are the objects through which user agency passes and is transformed into digital signals to be interpreted by software and hardware. Our onscreen identities or characters in a video game and our viewing preferences that we submit to a digital video recorder are all channeled through such controls. How, then, does the control or controller in the palm of one's hand shape the virtual engagements with identity that take place across both video games and television today?

CONTROLLING IDENTITY,
VIEWERSHIP, AND INTERACTIVITY

"Identity" in digital media culture is often understood through acts that dislocate embodied identity from the self online, and studies emphasize how such a dislocation enables one to enact multiple, contradictory identities. Other theorists have explored the identities that populate virtual worlds like Multi-User Dungeons/Dimensions (MUDs), and how those identities work through the selection and customization of a textually enacted persona.[8] By understanding digital identity as the virtualization of identity and as a form of free-for-all identity play, new media theorists risk, in Tara McPherson's words, "reinstalling a new millennial version of the 'universal subject' of 1970s film theory" (184). As Linda Williams notes in the introduction to *Viewing Positions: Ways of Seeing Film* (1995), the "universal subject" of 1970s film theory that focused upon the gaze was "both oversimplified and ahistorical" because such theories did not take into account the many different contexts in which cinema is viewed (3). Within new media studies, the diverse structures of new media technologies and experiences are just beginning to be uncovered. Indeed, arguments like Allucquère Rosanne Stone's influential and oft-cited 1991 essay, "Will the Real Body Please Stand Up?" focuses on the processes of virtualization and simulation involved in enacting identities through digital media, while overlooking the specificities and materialities that connect a digital identity—be it online or in a video game—to the user operating and orchestrating such a performance. Unfortunately, David Gauntlett's comments on academic explorations of identity are on target: very few theories of identity in new media culture tackle the ways that virtual identities are deeply connected to the nondigital world or present a more complicated model of identification that goes beyond a free fall of play and pseudonymity.

While playing a game, one must switch between embodying and controlling a character as an avatar and then passively watching the same character in a video game "cinematic" or "cut-scene" composed of an animated sequence that is watched in between active game-play (such scenes often include spoken dialogue between characters).[9] Since the 1990s, video and computer games have also been produced so that players may easily switch between different perspectival systems during game play. Whichever perspective a gamer chooses, he or she still remains in control of an avatar's actions and movements throughout much of the game.

According to the strictest definitions of the form, video games are those that are played on console systems connected to a television set, as opposed to PC or computer games played on a personal computer that may or may not be connected to the Internet. Essentially gaming computers and audio-visual entertainment systems, game consoles can also function as CD and DVD players. At present, the three dominant video game consoles are the Sony Playstation 3 (2006), the Microsoft Xbox 360 (2005), and the Nintendo Wii (2006). Computer games also contribute to the overall revenues and culture of gaming and are primarily designed to be played on PC clones (there are very few games designed for Apple computers), hence the designation "PC games" in most video and computer game lexicons. PC games share much with video games: aesthetics, game design/physics, and modes of interactivity, though there are certain genres that are more common to computer gaming than video gaming—like the controversial first-person shooter games that were originally designed for PCs and continue to thrive on that platform.[10]

At present, many games are released on multiple platforms simultaneously; a good example is the popular *Lord of the Rings: Fellowship of the Ring* (2002) game based on the film and book, released by Vivendi Universal, which can be played on a PC, a Sony Playstation 2, the Microsoft Xbox, or the handheld Nintendo Gameboy Advance. In certain instances, a game design studio will have an exclusive development deal with one video game console platform, as is the case with some of the titles in Rockstar Game's *Grand Theft Auto* series, which began as a PC game that lead to a sequel available on multiple systems, followed by an exclusive deal with Sony for Playstation 2 before more recent titles were again released for multiple platforms simultaneously.

The effects of multiple moving image modes and perspectives in contemporary video games upon a gamer's identification with a character and his or her "immersion" into the world of the game can be quite profound and can demonstrate how video game identity and identification works. These effects also demonstrate how this increasingly central domain of popular media builds upon the cinema as a cultural vernacular, as well as introducing a profoundly *physical* and sometimes aural element into the discourse of *"virtual* identities" within the emerging field of new media studies. Through the controller and game software, and increasingly via "live" audio components in multiplayer games, the gamer engages both the physical and virtual at once, rather than selecting the virtual over the physical, as earlier generations of technology enthusiasts and scholars believed one would have to do. Perhaps this physical object—the controller itself—needs to be approached not as a radical new mode of interactivity with television and the virtual worlds of video games, but as a continuation of an object that has been part of the history of television for decades.

In the underrated 1998 film *Pleasantville*, fraternal twins Jen (Reese Witherspoon) and David (Tobey Maguire) escape contemporary reality and enter into the sanitized 1950s world of David's favorite situation comedy, transported there by a magical remote control device provided to David by a mysterious TV repairman (Don Knotts, whose iconic status as a television star was, with a wink, on display in the film as well). Once back in the past, both twins learn valuable lessons applicable to their predicaments in the present. Of course they also radically affect the town of Pleasantville, bringing about both the civil rights movement and the beginnings of the sexual revolution. The film's reworking of history and the applicability of past historical struggles to contemporary problems is most problematically emblematized by Witherspoon's Jen, a teenage girl who chooses to remain in 1950s Pleasantville for the "opportunities" it offers her as a young woman, rather than return to present-day reality, where she believes her options are far more limited (how's that for historical revisionism?). David and Jen's journey into the television set and its generic world is diegetically put into motion by the technologies of TV themselves, particularly the remote control. Similar "magic" remotes serve as the deus ex machina in films as wide-ranging as *Being There* (Ashby, 1979), *Stay Tuned* (Hyams, 1992), and *Click* (Coraci, 2006). Through these filmic representations of television, the medium becomes a vehicle for personal change, and the remote is the tool that is used to make that change happen.

Remote control devices, which had first been attempted as a convenience device for radio listeners, have existed on the consumer television market since shortly after World War II, when television broadcasts penetrated the United States and television sets became reliably available for purchase (Bellamy and Walker 18–21) (see figure 16). In his reexamination of Raymond Williams's key work on televisual flow, William Uricchio introduces the terms "disruption" and "flow" to describe how contemporary television, not just accessed and organized through a remote control hardware device but also sorted and categorized by metadata tags and filters, doesn't simply "flow" from programs into commercials but is also part of a more complex circuit of contemporary information and delivery devices. Uricchio goes on to describe how the remote control device "stands in synergetic relation to the increase in broadcast channels, the availability of cable service, and the introduction of the VCR by serving to facilitate mobility among the 'older' broadcast forms and the 'newer' programming sources and by enabling the viewer to move among program forms with considerable ease. Most important, it signals a shift away from the programming-based notion of flow that Williams documented to a viewer-centered notion" ("Television's Next Generation" 168). With our remote controls in hand, we the viewers become the organizing "logic" of television today, particularly when utilizing "universal" remote controls that bring disparate technologies, information, and programming together under our command.

Uricchio's emphasis on the remote control device's ability to bridge old and new and shift the "control" of TV flows away from broadcasters and toward viewers, positions the remote control as a powerful tool for both disruption and control. Like the game controller, the remote control transfers interactivity and agency into the viewer's hands, even for transitory moments of "zapping" or "surfing" channels. The introduction of all-in-

16. A selection of remote control devices.

one "universal" remotes expand this agency to include control over the time one watches recorded content and even how long it takes to watch a program, since commercials and other elements can be paused, watched in fast-motion, or bypassed altogether. While some might argue that this is very minimal and rote interactivity, I believe the viewer's incorporation of the remote control device into the viewing experience signals a sustained and embodied aspect of TV spectatorship, just as the use of a game controller is integral to one's interactivity with a game. Today it is not uncommon for game controller devices to also include programmed remote control functionality, so that pressing a certain sequence of buttons on a Playstation 2 controller will activate and play a DVD in the Playstation 2's disc drive, allowing the gamer to switch modes from interactive user into digital video viewer. Whether or not the agency of the remote control and game controller is "false" is almost beside the point: what does happen when we use controllers and remote controls is that we physically and cognitively incorporate the digital device into our interactive experience of both old (TV) and new (video game) media. We extend ourselves through such controls and programs, and games reach out to us via these handheld gadgets as well. Such new media elements as these require greater extension, especially since remote controls can operate television receivers in multiple modes, expanding the "set" beyond its role as a vehicle for commercial content and into the realms of home cinema spectatorship and video gaming, as well as interacting with Internet content.

In a key passage in his critically acclaimed study *The Language of New Media (2001)*, Lev Manovich derisively criticizes the existing scholarship on new media and interactivity, proclaiming that such work mistakes *physical* interactivity for intellectual, thoughtful interaction. In doing so, Manovich, like many before him, falls into the "old Cartesian trap of separating the mind from the body." Manovich writes: "When we use the concept of 'interactive media' exclusively in relation to computer-based media, there is the danger that we will interpret 'interaction' literally, equating it with physical interaction between a user and a media object (pressing a button, choosing

a link, moving the body), at the expense of psychological interaction" (57).

Yet psychological interaction begins and ends with the physical interaction of the body, because when the subject views or
interacts with media, he or she does so from a specific historical
and cultural context and as the occupant of a specific materiality
(body). Later in *The Language of New Media*, Manovich goes
on to discuss video and computer games as exemplary new
media objects, but in doing so he mostly abandons questions of
how identification functions in regard to new media, creating
a telling absence in his text, especially since he provocatively
declares that, "Interactive media ask us to identify with someone
else's mental structure" (61).[11] In discussing video game identity and television viewer agency, one can uncover some of
these "mental structures" put in place by TV and video game
hardware designers and game programmers, and also how one's
navigation and play constitute a deeply embodied experience
of digital media identities.

Video game culture has been historically dominated by
amateur historians, fanboys, and media geeks[12]—those who
love games and gaming—while scholars have historically paid
scant attention to video games. The academic field of video
game studies has emerged over the past several years through
a publishing boom in game studies, as well as numerous
conferences dedicated to the past, present, and future of game
cultures. Much of the popular press attention to gaming
continues to focus on its perceived negative media effects,
like the psychological and sociological aspects of games and
children's use of the medium, or as part of the ongoing
discourse on video game violence.[13] As a new field, video
game studies has a rich terrain to cover with broad historical,
aesthetic and cultural implications. Since about 2000, this has
begun to change, with a rush of new, critical video game
publications, including Mark J. P. Wolf's *The Medium of the
Video Game* (2001); Ian Bogost's *Unit Operations: An Approach
to Video Game Criticism* (2006), Wolf and Bernard Perron's
The Video Game Theory Reader (2003) and *Video Game Theory
Reader 2* (2009), Jesper Juul's explorations of rules and casual

gaming in *Half-Real: Video Games between Real Rules and Fictional Worlds* (2005) and *A Casual Revolution: Reinventing Video Games and Their Players* (2009), as well as Steve Jones's literary theory–inspired approach to the topic in *The Meaning of Video Games: Gaming and Textual Strategies* (2008). These works, representing a wide range of academic disciplines, including film and media studies, technology studies, critical theory, and others, indicate how wide and interdisciplinary the study of video games is and can be for scholars who are open to analyzing these interactive texts, systems, and industries.

The input devices in contemporary video game systems have controls mapped to perform a range of different functions and are designed so that they ergonomically fit within a player's hands. Controllers also have a range of buttons (buttons, joysticks, digital, analog) and these inputs/buttons function differently in different games.[14] Nearly the entire surface of a video game controller for a system like Playstation 3 or Xbox 360 is taken up by buttons and analog sticks that allow a gamer to perform multiple simultaneous tasks while playing (see figure 17). Meanwhile, the "Wiimote" controller for the Nintendo Wii invokes the design of the remote control in its name, button layout, and shape, which looks like the familiar form of a television remote control but has added functions for gaming.

Forcing Feedback: Game Controls

Contemporary home gaming system controllers include force feedback motors—variously called "dualshock," "rumble motors," or "vibration feedback motors"—these devices work to make a gamer feel the repercussions of his or her actions and inactions within a game. According to Nintendo, the company that introduced this technology to the home market in 1997 with its Nintendo RumblePak accessory for the N64 gaming system, a force feedback motor is "a device that physically responds to the action in compatible games, immersing you in the game play."[15] When I am unable to hit the correct buttons fast enough and in the proper sequence,

17. A Sony Playstation 2 controller.

my avatar in a game may lose a fight or run into a wall, but I will also experience a secondary version of the consequences as the controller shakes, vibrates, and even jolts wildly in my hands. Indeed, Sony includes a disclaimer in their Playstation 2 manual that reads: "The vibration function of the analog controller (Dualshock2) . . . can aggravate injuries. Do not use the vibration function of the analog controller . . . if you have any ailment in the bones or joints of your hands or arms."

Tellingly, with the extremely successful launch of Nintendo's innovative Wii video game system and "wiimote," concerns arose about new types of "wiinjuries" like repetitive stress injuries and (virtual) tennis elbow. Handheld devices and leisure activities like gaming often come under scrutiny when a new technological form like the Wiimote is so rapidly and broadly successful. Of course more recent video game titles, such as *Wii Fit* (2008), *EA Sports Active* (2009), and *Jillian Michaels Fitness Ultimatum 2010* (2009) are made with the explicit intention of game play affecting the gamer's body as part of a fitness program. Now television can be used to reshape and change its viewers' bodies by activating them and engaging them in virtual play. The results are measured by game system components that serve multiple purposes. For instance, the Wii Balance Board is also a digital scale.

"LET'S DO THIS TOGETHER NOW!": VIDEO GAMES AND TV REMAKE YOUR BODY

In combination with the three-dimensional graphics of the games played on these home gaming systems, force feedback motors are designed to make the virtual experiences of games more immersive and more experiential, yet when I play, as well as feeling as if I am drawn more deeply into the game, I also notice how the game is, increasingly, spilling outside of its digital space and onto the physical space in which I play, as well as onto my body.[16] My lived space is saturated with and changed by the events occurring within a game and to my avatar. And this is exactly the kind of experience game designers want players to have. For instance, Microsoft promotes its Xbox system as superior gaming hardware that "empowers game artists by giving them the technology to fulfill their creative visions as never before, creating games that blur the lines between fantasy and reality." Reality isn't "left behind" by games, but it is reformatted.

When designing a game, designers and programmers map out how the video game system input devices will function with the physics of the virtual environments rendered in a game. Paired with force feedback motors and the perspectival system I mentioned earlier—the ways in which many games allow one to easily shift between third-person and first-person perspectives—a video game's controls become essential to the player's experience of a game and his or her ability to identify with the avatar he or she is operating. Like switching viewpoints, gamers oscillate between identifying with and responding to their avatars and other characters in a game.

While playing a game, as when watching television with a remote control, the user enters into a complicated play with not only his or her identity but also with his or her body and its McLuhanesque "extensions" and tools. When one engages with digital media, such modifications certainly take place—although no one "true" identity is uncovered *or* left behind in the process. In the case of video games, identity is most substantially modified by the ways that users can control their digital proxies—and also in the ways that they surrender control over themselves and their characters in order to play.[17]

This is a new media television experience—a moment of new media reinventing TV beyond its capacity to display network channels or carry cable signals, as Ralph Baer's quote at the start of this chapter suggests. This moment of reinventing and expanding television is also a key moment for the invention of the home video game system. It is not, however, strictly speaking, an easy instance of media convergence. I cannot watch a television program and play a game of *Super Mario Brothers Wii* (2009) simultaneously on one television set. In the opposite way, standing on my Wii Balance Board while watching television will not increase my fitness level or indicate to me how much I weigh: one mode cancels the other out. Instead, I switch between and among the multitude of new media modes accessible through my television set. In this way, then, the gamer/viewer truly is the central logic and "switching" station that disrupts and controls television's flow.

In David Cronenberg's nightmarish video game opus, *eXistenZ*, the film's characters and spectators must navigate a dizzying array of game worlds and storylines, leading one character to proclaim, at the very end of the film, "Hey, tell me the truth . . . are we still in the game?" In the world of *eXistenZ*, this is a valid question. The game worlds are connected to the real world in a multitude of physical (spinal) connections between human bodies and bio-port gaming consoles that plug into one's body, infecting it with the virus of gaming. Once a body has been ported and opened up to the game, it, as in many of Cronenberg's films, also opens up to new realities, ones in which the boundaries between bodies and technologies are thoroughly blurred. This filmic re-presentation of video games as simulated reality-shifting devices foregrounds how game spaces are increasingly embodied spaces—even if only in the fictional realm. But, as I have shown, contemporary games also perform a similar shift: making the virtual space of the game—of the television set itself—into an embodied space.

When Sony suggests that its customers "Live in your world, play in ours," this is not an either/or suggestion. One *both* lives in his or her world while also playing in Sony's Playstation world. These spaces overlap one another and are linked through the screen and the console of the gaming system. The in-game structures that enables the identification of the gamer with the on-screen character—perspectival modes, narration, cinematics, audio cues, force feedback, densely orchestrated game levels and worlds—all serve to deepen the connection between the game world and the real world. And this is exactly what makes gaming so appealing to gamers and so dangerous in the eyes of media reformers and censors. Perhaps it is also what marks gaming as separate from the typical discourse surrounding television and its networks, channels, and formats.

DANCE, DANCE REVOLUTION: VIRTUAL AND ACTUAL MOVEMENT

Arcade and home video game versions of the popular game *Dance, Dance Revolution* (*DDR* 1998) require the player to progress through the game by copying dance steps seen on screen, all to the beat of contemporary popular music. Unlike the typical computer or video game, interaction between the user and the machine is much more corporealized in a game like *DDR* or its offshoots and copycats. You must dance to play: refuse to move and lose the game. One needs more than a hand motivating a mouse, joystick, or button. Actual movement is a huge part of the game—as evidenced by sweaty participants and workout games based on the aerobic activity and success of *DDR*. As soon as Nintendo's much anticipated Wii system launched, so did Wii-based workout programs, produced by enthusiastic fans and gamers who had adapted their love for their games to their need for physical activity.

DDR is so popular—so ubiquitous as both a challenging game and as a casual (bar, pub, arcade) activity for nongamers— that indie-pop singer John Vanderslice toyed with the game in his 2005 song "Exodus Damage." Teasing with the implied "revolution" of the game's title, Vanderslice invokes actual chaos, rather than dancing, as he sings of the fall of the World Trade Center on September 11, 2001:

dance dance revolution
all we're gonna get
unless it falls apart
so I say: go go go
let it fall down
I'm ready for the end

Here, *DDR* is more than a game, it is a metaphor for contemporary, mediated life.

Like *DDR*, the Nintendo Wii requires users to become more physically engaged with its programs than previous gaming systems (see figure 18). This trend, finally arriving a decade after virtual reality enthusiasts hoped it would, engages media users as embodied subjects rather than enticing them to enter into a disembodied virtual cyberspace in which subjectivity is aligned with the mind and not the body. Yet it is not so simple as a mind/body split. Theorists like N. Katherine Hayles and Vivian Sobchack have shown in their work how virtuality trips up, doubles, and confuses mind–body dualities.

As the preceding discussion of controllers and remotes, force feedback, user interactivity, and immersion has indicated, such identification fuses the user's physical and virtual experiences to the onscreen representation and its world. Whereas early theorists of new media were quick to recognize that interactivity is shot through with great potentiality, one can now see that negotiating and using new media is often about switching modes and making trade-offs: will I sacrifice interaction to engage in a closed but satisfying narrative experience? Will I watch one, two, or three programs "at once," deftly switching between them? Do I prioritize real-time responsiveness or contemplative, turn-based logic? Do I want to play with this media alone, with virtual surrogates or with other, actual users located in my own physical space or remotely connected to the same media network I am using?

18. A gamer plays an "upper body" game from *Active Life Outdoor Challenge* on the Nintendo Wii. (Photograph by Jean Leverich, used with permission.)

Where do I look to for these experiences? My television set? My video game system? Both? My computer or perhaps some jury-rigged, Rube Goldberg–esque combination that conjoins my new media together, allowing me to switch between and among television, gaming, the Internet, virtual simulations, and active, physical engagements?

If there is one thing that is true about media convergence, it is rarely as smooth and streamlined as advertisements lead us to believe it is. Instead, as I have witnessed, domestic instances of convergence as they take place in a contemporary family room require skilled uses of multiple technologies. These spaces, which no longer house just a television set, hi-fi, and family gathered round them, are inherently multifunctional in contemporary culture, housing the work and play of media use. Today's middle-class family room is often also home to multiple gaming systems, broadband routers, digital video recorders, digital video disc players, cable boxes, speaker sets, and oversized pieces of furniture designed to contain DVD cases, CDs, books, and tools. On the side table sits mobile phones, chargers, three or four remote controls, and nearby are laptop bags and stands. Clearly not every living room looks like this imagined one. Yet—and here is where the "ALT-CTRL" of this chapter's title comes into play—most domestic and many work spaces today do perform multiple functions. On a personal computer, hitting the "ALT-CTRL" key simultaneously allows the keyboard to function differently than it does in its standard mode—these are short-cut keys allowing computer users more control over the technology. PC gamers are quite familiar with ALT-CTRL and other keyboard shortcuts that enable them to play faster and respond more accurately to a game. But, using the keyboard or not, many people today alternate and control the new media around them using a variety of strategies, including the arrangement of technologies in the home.

My imagined living room—an interior decorator's nightmare to be sure—typifies how many new media elements routinely circulate in daily life.[18] And yet, despite the addition of TiVos, Uverses, Xboxes, Wiis, Playstations, DVD players, mobile devices, and laptop computers, the central screen in the room, the device around which all these technologies are centered and that they are designed to interact with and upon, is the television screen. It is still there as a central element of new media. TV continues to bring together and, even, at times, offer up moments of control over new media experience today.

Television Is
Not New Media

In the cities in which we live, all of us see
hundreds of publicity images every day of
our lives. No other kind of image confronts
us so frequently. . . . Publicity speaks in the
future tense and yet the achievement of this
future is endlessly deferred.

—John Berger, *Ways of Seeing*

THIS CONCLUSION is a departure from the
previous chapters, in that it describes new screen technologies that are not fully in place and whose uses are still being
determined. Although video technologies and brand logos
often encountered on traditional television sets are part of this
discourse, the development and use of interactive video systems
designed for physical engagement opens up questions that go
beyond television. Perhaps these systems are, in some infini-
tesimal way, a kind of offspring of the convergence between
television and new media, though the very biological premise
of that framework troubles me. Still, as this book seeks to define
both television and new media through one another, systems like
these must be considered as the next possible step new media
might take.

In *1984*, George Orwell described a future where
walls were also screens—a video architecture that surveilled
domestic space while relaying state programming and
government information to those inside of it. Such full-

scale video architecture does not exist today outside of the domain of installation art or in stand-alone video advertising screens and billboards. Yet what would happen if television screens expanded and became part of the built environment as moving image structures? In the emerging field of interactive advertising, television screens and short commercial advertisements have given way to large surfaces displaying projected, interactive programming. These commercial interactive video installations take the "alt-ctrl" aspects of video gaming discussed in chapter four and turn the human body into the game controller itself, while the television set recedes into a flexible, nondescript media surface designed to display images and encourage physical engagement.

Today (at 186 locations in thirty major advertising markets) you can walk into the multiplex, the mall, the airport, or other contemporary nonspaces, and you will encounter such an installation. The focus here is primarily on systems produced by Reactrix, but there are a handful of other companies exploring similar technologies.[1] The Reactrix advertising system projects interactive digital moving pictures onto the surface of the floor and often attracts children (the youngest consumers) and their parents. The company boasts on their Web site that they make "over 100 million impressions a month" with their systems, which constantly recombine bright images that shift and morph, creating kinetic puzzles and groupings one can trigger and change through physical movement.[2] Systems like Reactrix necessitate a reconsideration as a well as a reconfiguration of the relationship between cinematic, virtual, consumptive, spatial, and embodied experience. Writing in 1972, John Berger did not imagine that our urban, industrialized "ways of seeing" would include interactive, gesturally responsive advertising systems. Yet his choice of the active verb "confront" to describe how publicity (advertising) images address "spectator-buyers" is telling and even seems prognostic in retrospect. Image systems like Reactrix do indeed "confront" us, calling upon users and consumers to confront them, (to react) right back.

AT THE THRESHOLD

But before approaching such screen-based interactive systems, one must first understand how these interactive imaging/advertising systems work. Reaxtrix's CEO Mike Ribero has referred to the system as a form of "visual karaoke" and "advertainment," and venture capitalist Heidi Roizen says, "It's something that changes the perception of the ad and makes it into an experience."[3] The system, which costs several thousand dollars to install, consists of a ceiling mounted rig with a PC, video projector, two sets of infrared motion sensor cameras, and an imaging system, along with a six-foot-by-eight-foot floor pad that users step, stomp, dance upon, and wave at to activate the motion control sensors and trigger video content. This content typically takes the form of animated, somewhat realistic graphical games. Through playing the game, users usually interact with a brand or product and its logo, though Reactrix also includes several game sequences that are simply visual encounters with no sell-through point—one can virtually "splash" through a koi pond and "touch" the fish or follow a basketball-sized white mouse through a maze to a piece of cheese at the center, which, once reached, disappears to reveal the Reactrix logo.[4]

As of mid-2008, the company's branding partners/advertisers included Coca-Cola, Clorox, Hilton, CBS, Sprint, Universal Studios, Visa, Wells Fargo, eBay, and Xbox, and in January 2008 Reactrix announced and demonstrated a second system called WAVEscape that is now in development with Samsung. WAVEscape was designed to have a more traditional positioning of its video elements on screens hung like small billboards in public spaces, but the screens have built-in motion control systems, and they will activate and change as consumers approach them. Like the current floor system, WAVEscape is what the company calls a "gesture-activated advertising and information screen" suitable for "malls, retail stores, and hotels."[5] This gesture-activated system is refined to the point where it can recognize a hand as a distinct body part, as well as a consumer's wave at the screen. For enthusiasts of new media technology, these are key developments—a responsive media system in which real movements trigger a chain of virtual, image- and sound-based responses. Perhaps WAVEscape is just another chapter in our ongoing pursuit of what André Bazin called "total cinema" or what Bolter and Grusin (among others) have referred to as immediacy and transparency in new media.[6]

Although there are a number of ways to approach and understand this technology, one must look at how Reactrix activates and changes the spaces into which it is installed and the uniquely embodied form of virtuality it offers. With Reactrix, there are no VR goggles or headsets, not even a handheld remote like one used in the rightfully lauded Nintendo Wii system. Instead, while waiting for the movie to start or, as the dozens of online images and clips of the system as well as my own casual mall ethnography has shown, while trying to entertain toddlers at the mall, Reactrix allows consumers to be their own input device. One moves back and forth across the floor screen, effectively turning the body into a computer mouse. The system, of course, is simply generating its images on demand as programmed, in this case to create brand awareness while the users are typically just playing or passing time in public spaces, with different designations, such as the mall (shopping) or multiplex (movie-going).[7] Though technologically quite different, systems like Reactrix are part of a larger cultural turn toward casual gaming on personal computers, phones, and other "smart" devices.

As I have argued elsewhere, new media technologies designed to fill "downtime" have a unique relationship to space. In his analysis of the spaces where one encounters video games, Raiford Guins discusses what he calls "threshold gaming"—the early appearance of video game cabinets in decidedly nonvideo game venues during the height of the arcade gaming craze of the late 1970s–early 1980s. Guins describes threshold games as those that are played in "the transitory, nondescript and virtually invisible space" outside of arcades and bars—airports, Laundromats, and so forth (204). Interactive media systems like Reactrix operate in a similar manner to the way that those early video arcade games did, reconfiguring seemingly transient passageways into zones for interaction (albeit usually interaction with a particular brand of consumer product). As Guins puts it, "Hidden in banality—in the void between the exit and checkout registers in grocery and convenience stores—the physical presence of arcade games configures social space into a televisual place" (204). Note that Guins still describes these spaces where video games were found as televisual, despite being public, banal locations.

I first became interested in interactive imaging systems after I'd had the somewhat disconcerting experience of walking underneath the Reactrix system at my mall several times, not sure why there was a video projector pointed at the floor as I tried to negotiate the crowded corridor. I was fairly certain that there wasn't a new installation video piece in town that had gotten permission to mount a huge projector on the ceiling, but it wasn't until I happened to be at the mall on a less crowded day that I could see how Reactrix invited shoppers to stop and play awhile and, in doing so, to uncover the Coca-Cola corporate logo. In the Ann Arbor mall the system is (I assume) strategically placed right in front of the BabyGap, where it is best situated to capture the attention of children and their upscale-demographic parents. And there, in front of the BabyGap or, as the other local system is set up, in front of the multiplex concession stand, Reactrix attempts to shift consumers momentarily out of the everyday space of the mall or multiplex and into its space of representation. (I should mention that, although the Reactrix games are short they do in fact require focused attention and interaction.) Spaces like these, newly embedded with video screens and inviting users to engage, are useful for understanding contemporary experience. Or, as Anna McCarthy puts it in *Ambient Television*: "The routine implantation of screens in transit stations, banks, and waiting rooms—the precise arenas in which these banal and repetitive gestures take place—would seem to be a crucial phenomenon for assessing the nature and direction of a politics of public space and the everyday" (7).

And indeed, Reactrix is designed to call the attention of consumers back to advertising at a time when more traditional forms of in-home screen advertising, like television spot ads, are in a state of crisis due to the changes brought about by digital video recorders and viewers' delight at the ability to scan through or skip over advertising altogether. As Reactrix CEO Michael Ribero puts it, the technology is intended for "any environment where people don't rush in and necessarily rush out."[8] Faced with an extra ten or fifteen minutes before your movie starts, would you rather watch the projected slide show of recycled movie trivia or play a game in which you virtually pour buckets of paint over the Visa logo or stomp out snowflakes that obscure the Coca-Cola sign? As the Reactrix corporate Web site asserts, "Brand play beats brand talk every time."

Interestingly, much of this "brand play" is evidence of a return to advertising that is largely based on the iconography or logo of a brand rather than on a high-concept, narrativized "brand image." With Reactrix one plays soccer across a field with the Wells Fargo logo in the middle or walk across a row of Xbox 360 consoles, activating a different skin or front-piece for each as you go. Most of these game-ads are premised upon consumers already having a set of associations with the brand being sold, freeing the game and gameplay elements to simply provide colorful and fun interaction ("Look at me! I made the bubbles disappear!"). By using Reactrix, we are positioning ourselves for the brand, just as the brand is being newly repositioned for us. To quote Ribero again, "People who buy products are advocates, critics, creators." Really? We are creators as we uncover the Coke logo? Of what?

Or, perhaps another productive way to approach the relationship between images and their users found in Reactrix is through a model like the one that artist and critic Ron Burnett develops in his book, *How Images Think* (2004). In this attempt to account for how the concepts, metaphors about, and actual flow of images have become central tropes in contemporary culture, Burnett explains how "Images are the interfaces that structure interaction, people, and the environments they share" (xix).[9] With systems like Reactrix, this interface is literally a structure that attempts to shift our relationship to the spaces it occupies so that we can play inside and with the image and the advertisement.

REACTRIX AND
EMBODIED VIRTUALITY

When one does play inside and upon Reactrix images, one also experiences a deeply embodied engagement with the virtual imagery generated by the system's imaging software. Increasingly, new media has offered up a kind of craze for such physical interactions with virtual, time-based media, as evidenced by the popularity of Nintendo's Wii gaming system and games like *Dance, Dance Revolution, Guitar Hero* (2006), and *Rock Band* (2007). And, although the easy answer to why so many gamers want to play games where they are virtual rock gods is that gamers really do want to be rock gods, there is some evidence that suggests other meanings can be derived from the experience of virtually "rocking out" along with your game console. In the 2007 "Guitar Queer-o" episode of *South Park*, Stan's father mistakes his son's obsession with the extremely popular Xbox video game *Guitar Hero* for a desire to actually play the guitar, and then tries to show off his legitimate guitar skills to the boys, who are quickly embarrassed by his actions. In a typically childish and homophobic *South Park* way, their exchange goes something like this:

STAN: Dad? Dad! What are you doing?!
RANDY: I can actually play a lot of these songs on a real guitar. You want me to teach you boys how?
CARTMAN: Uhh, that's gay, Mr. Marsh.
STAN: Yeah, that's stupid, Dad.
RANDY: But . . . But this is real.
CARTMAN: Real guitars are for old people.[10]

In "Guitar Queer-o," "real" skills are for the old, while virtual and simulated skills are the domain of the young. Although *South Park* is not a direct barometer of public sentiment, at the moment there does seem to be both a desire for mastering the interaction necessitated by a physically engaged game like *Guitar Hero* (where the controller is a guitar with flat button inputs) and a fascination with engaging in virtual play in embodied, active ways. (Later in the episode both Stan and his dad become addicted to *Guitar Hero* and then are advised to play the "even more addictive" game *Heroin Hero*, which Stan can only get out of his system by reverting to the less complex, repetitive video game genre of driving simulations.)

However, Reactrix does offer up a tamer and less determined version of such embodied virtual experiences because these games are short and transitory and are situated in spaces where they operate as a kind of threshold. Reactrix offers up the physical engagement of a Wii or dance game with none of the fiscal or long-term commitment that those other systems require. Perhaps such physically motivated systems are an important new direction for consumer-level digital media, or perhaps they are just the latest fad—it is far too soon to tell.

When I teach about virtual reality systems in my Introduction to New Media class I often begin with a scene from the feature film (and feature-length Nintendo advertisement) *The Wizard* (Holland, 1989). In it, the film's protagonist, a video game wunderkind, faces his nemesis. The bad guy gets his secret weapon out of a special briefcase, in a climactic moment leading up to the big, Western-style showdown between the two opponents. The secret weapon is Nintendo's Powerglove, one of the only virtual reality products to actually make it to the consumer market from the 1990s VR craze. The Powerglove depends upon technology developed by *Mondo 2000* cover boy Jaron Lanier and VPL Research, leaders in the early 1990s virtual reality craze. Even so, the Powerglove was always more "vapor" than ware: only two games were ever released that were designed for use with this input device.[11] I show the scene in class because it so aptly demonstrates the hype and mystique often accorded to new technologies. When the Powerglove appears onscreen, held up in a specially padded, steel suitcase, it always fails to thrill my contemporary audience. The dissipation of the once-powerful aura of technological mystery and mastery that the Powerglove supposedly had is even more apparent when viewed just sixteen years or so after the film's release. I wonder, what will be the Powerglove of this new media era? Will we always be entranced by digital promises of embodied engagement through and beyond what our screens can offer? Will we still think of television when we see large scale video screens, video walls, video floors?

TELEVISION IS NOT NEW MEDIA; OR, MOVING FROM A "WINDOW TO THE WORLD" TO WORLDS IN WINDOWS

Writing in 1946 in the prologue to a colleague's newly published text, New York University professor Paul McGhee tried to summarize television's potential impact on society, just as TV was finally becoming a viable consumer technology. I am going to quote McGhee's prose, which runs long, because I think it gives some sense of the scope of TV's impact as a new technology:

> The author of this book has helped to shape the beginnings of television, the newest of the instruments available to those in the future who seek to inform the minds of men, or to win their sympathy and understanding. It takes imagination and daring to leave the security of a known medium, to explore, through trial and error, with tools which are often anachronisms as soon as used, a new medium which has a limited audience, no traditions, no certainties of technique. . . . In television we have instrument which can make possible our identification with our fellow men over the face of the earth. We shall hear them speak to us and see them clearly in their appeal for understanding. They will see and hear us, and we must make them know our purposes. This has been possible through the newsreel but television will make the immediacy of the relationship beyond escape. . . . Those who work in magazines, in books, in radio, in motion pictures, in television, hold our tomorrow in their hands. (v–vii)[12]

McGhee's preface is filled with hope and optimism—about the future possibilities surrounding the new technology of television for our identification with others, for the immediacy of the medium, and for the emergence of new forms of communication. Today it is hard to see TV from the perspective of someone from 1946. And yet, if we fast-forward forty-five years and read architect Michael Benedikt's early analysis of virtual reality environments and communities, there are echoes of McGhee's optimism about new technologies. Benedikt writes: "On the experiential front, our lives are changing too. Ever more dependent upon channels of communication, ever more saturated by the media, ever more reliant on the vast traffic in invisible data and ever more connected to the computers that manage it, we are becoming each day divided more starkly into the entertainers and the entertained, the informationally adept and the informationally inept.... Under these new conditions, the definition of reality itself has become uncertain. New forms of literacy and new means of orientation are called for."[13]

It is, perhaps, unfair to juxtapose one author's take on television, seen now from a historical distance and read with regards to the passage of time, with another's proclamations about the emergence of cyberspace and virtual realities that was written much closer to our own moment. Yet, the words of Paul McGhee, New York University Professor of Education and Dean in 1946 and architect Michael Benedikt's remarks from 1991 both speak to the rush of expectations and hopes placed upon each new media in its time. These media will teach us, and, McGhee writes in his postwar urgency, help us understand others across the globe. They will entail new literacies and accommodations to the onslaught of data, just as they will divide us according to who can make new media and who can use it—and who won't get to do either of those things. Yet these descriptions of the new mediums of television and virtual reality both speak to the broader social aims and mandates that are often placed upon technological, communications advances, as discussed earlier in this book. To conclude, then, I want to look at a software program that has emerged and been rhetorically framed in ways reminiscent of television and the early Internet. Google Earth puts the "vision at a distance" part of television into a whole new context outside our own globe. At the same time, we can understand this software as yet another new "window on the world," echoing early television programming by NBC and later theories by Marshall McLuhan and others.

Finally, I will return to that time-space-distance origami first folded and unfolded in the introduction by considering just how one writes about the new and the present, through an examination of Chris Marker's hauntingly beautiful anthropological essay film *Sans Soleil* (1982). First, though, one must encounter the alarmingly easy, intuitive, and powerful interface of Google Earth and its model of global visuality.

In 2005, Google, Inc., introduced Google Earth, a new software program that the company had acquired from Keyhole, Inc. Unlike many other Google software tools, Google Earth is a stand-alone software program operated separately from one's Internet browser, but it is designed to work on most contemporary computer systems, with versions available for a wide range of operating system platforms. The program that the Keyhole software architects had built is a "virtual globe, map, and geographic information program,"[14] or, as Google's own Web site puts it, Google Earth is "the world's geographic information at your fingertips."[15] Yet even this description, promising to put world geography at one's fingertips, minimizes the experience and visualities encountered by users of the software. Google Earth 5.0, released in February 2009, allows users to access oceanographic maps and underwater terrain data, as well as to leave Earth behind to visit Google Mars, made from a compilation of high-resolution images from Mars lander. Google Earth 5.0 users can also, in a special software release timed to match the fortieth anniversary of the *Apollo 11* mission, spend time on Google Moon.

Much like the interface of the virtual world *Second Life*, in Google Earth the user can "jump" or "fly" across vast geographic distances—spinning the globe while simultaneously zooming into one's destination. Unlike *Second Life*, in Google Earth one is simply represented by an arrow or cursor, not an avatar. Clearly we are meant to be our (nonvirtual) selves sitting at the computer as we use this tool rather than engage with it as simulations of our self. The focus is not on who is doing the exploring and looking but solely on the views that the software provides—there are uploaded photos for many locations in addition to satellite photography and layers of map data. Intuitively designed and highly responsive—a simple click will generate a zoom or movement—Google Earth is easy and fun to use, just like the similar Google Maps program accessed through a Web browser.

Using the Google Earth software is a nearly perfect exercise in the new media modality of remediation so aptly theorized by Richard Grusin and J. David Bolter in their book *Remediation: Understanding New Media* (1999). Written in the late 1990s at a time of increases in network bandwidth and the rise of commercial uses of Internet technologies, Bolter and Grusin described the World Wide Web as an emerging, major (virtual) locus for media distribution and use. Their theory of remediation argued that new media is marked by its "dual logics" of hypermediacy and immediacy, as well as by its tendency to simultaneously strive for hypermediacy and immediacy together. Hypermediacy refers to the tendency of contemporary digital media to call attention repeatedly and consistently to its own status as media, something we encounter today in everything from the now-standard cable news screen "crawl" of information along the bottom of our screens to the proliferation of heavily fetishized, high-design media players and mobile phones, which are hypermediated via both their software interfaces and their design aesthetic (34).

But just what connects a piece of software like Google Earth to the medium of television? To find this connection, we must turn to the concept of the window, or, more precisely, the "virtual window" as theorized by film scholar Anne Friedberg.[16] Friedberg deftly traces out a history and theory of the window as architectural element, metaphor, and functional frame through which space and time are perceived. As she puts it, "the window has a deep cultural history as an architectural and figurative trope for the framing of the pictorial image" (5). Windows, then, are the metaphoric register under which both television and computer screens are described and understood. Although neither the TV set nor the computer screen functions as an actual architectural aperture, both are virtual windows that frame the views they contain and present. To quote Friedberg, "recent televisual features (programming style cluttered with text crawls and inset frames; monitors enabled with 'picture in picture' display) facilitate multiple-screen insets, televisual 'windows' have become multiple and simultaneous receivers of a variety of programming" (193). At the same time when television's "windows on the world" have incorporated new infotainment elements, the window of the computer screen is literally marked as a trademarked "window" by the dominant graphical user interface and operating system of the personal computer industry—Microsoft's Windows. The style and functionality of Microsoft's point-and-click interface has in fact become a synecdoche for a graphical user interface.[17]

In the 1950s, the National Broadcasting Corporation (NBC) explicitly invited this comparison of the television set and television studio with the window through the design and in-show function of architectural windows on their morning news magazine program *The Today Show* (1952–present). *The Today Show*'s "windows on the world" are both architecture *and* metaphor, and were designed to engage passersby with the studio and its broadcasts.[18] As architecture, the street-level floor-to-ceiling windows gave crowds on the street a view into Rockefeller Center and *The Today Show* set, cameras, and production equipment. Standing in the crowd gathered outside the studio, one is both "behind the scenes" of the show and a live element of the show's scenery—a "special effect," as it were, of the live audience mirrored by those watching through their televisual "windows" at home. In fact, when NBC built a new studio for the show in 1994, its architectural plan referenced the early 1950s set and its oversized, street-level windows. The NBC Web site even boasts, "The three-story, 18,000-square-foot home of 'Today' now attracts thousands of visitors each year to peer into its windows and become part of 'Today''s broadcast."[19] As is so often the case with television, viewers and their encounter with the world via windows, both real and virtual, become part of the spectacle itself.

WINDOWS AND GLOBES,
NOT MIRRORS

This sense of the TV window being an opening unto the world beyond one's immediate physical grasp is also part of what such phraseology invokes. Indeed, the NBC Web site goes on to shift its focus from the studio's architectural windows to the metaphoric "window on the world": "'Today' is also renowned for providing its audience with a window on the world by broadcasting from remote locations around the globe. The program has originated from Africa, China, the Soviet Union, France, Italy, the United Kingdom and Ireland, Australia, South America, Cuba, and aboard the Orient Express."[20]

Invoking an armchair traveler logic that is often reiterated within advertisements about digital media technologies, *The Today Show* promises to bring the viewer at home, drinking morning coffee, into contact with far-flung sites and exotic encounters with cultures both distant and difficult to access on one's own. Companies from AT&T to CISCO (a company that designs and manufactures network routers) have also worked this same angle, depicting their technologies as the bridge that fills the gap between East and West, young and old, male and female, rich and poor. Such advertising usually involves a montage that depicts a vast range of people (I often joke that somehow these ads typically include Buddhist monks using laptops as part of the anachronistic cultures brought together via new media) and a unifying slogan like AT&T's "You Will" campaign from the early 1990s ("Have you ever studied with a classmate thousands of miles away? You Will. And the company that will bring it to you is AT&T."), or CISCO's "Human Network" advertisements from 2006–2009, which simply show a set of evocative images brought to the consumer by CISCO, the Human Network. Both campaigns distinctly avoid promoting particular products or services, instead promoting an overall technological solution that the brand can supply.

Most crucially for my purposes here, though, is the way this solution is visually represented as "global"—a multiethnic, multicultural human exchange of community, education, and productivity. All good stuff, right? This sense of the global, opened up to us by our windows on the world, is a far cry from the global trade in pornography that actually led to the increased bandwidth which we now routinely utilize to form virtual communities, educate ourselves, or act as productive citizens of the world.[21] Beginning with the televisual notion of the "window to and on the world" and picked up by corporations invested in the network infrastructure of the Internet, one can see how both television and computers have rhetorically figured as windows on the world. On top of that, both television and computers have been the locus of another enduring metaphor for communications technology, the global village, a community made possible by the virtual cultural encounters that television and computers enable.

Like the literal and metaphoric "windows on the world" provided by both television and networked computers, these technologies have also been rhetorically linked to the concept of the "global village" first described by Marshall McLuhan in 1962.[22] In McLuhan's account, which he describes at length in *Understanding Media: The Extensions of Man* (1964), the global village is technologically produced by the unifying power of electricity, satellite, and broadcast technologies.[23] Through our engagement with television and telecommunications, we are "retribalized" as members of the electronic global village. As McLuhan puts it, "We are no more prepared to encounter radio and TV in our literate milieu than the native of Ghana is able to cope with the literacy that takes him out of his collective tribal world and beaches him in individual isolation. We are as numb in our new electric world as the native involved in our literate and mechanical culture" (207).[24]

Replete with primitivist tropes and described in colonizing language that assumes tribalism is equivalent with collectivity, McLuhan's description of the global village also characterize it as a great equalizer; encounters with the technological render everyone "numb," just as the globe itself is shrunk into a village it is only possible to visit via television (or now, computer networks). Elsewhere in *Understanding Media*, McLuhan celebrated the worldwide gatherings made possible by television's "electronic hearth": a global village enabled a planetary "technological embrace" around the television set, with the technology determining and synergistically effacing political, social, and economic differences among viewers of mass spectacle. *The Today Show* knows how to work this global village rhetoric, as it promises home viewers a window into communist Cuba or a ride on the Orient Express.

Don't Forget the View
from Your Windows

How, then, have these virtual windows opened up such rich apertures, such opportunities to visit faraway places without leaving our couches or La-Z-boys? One way is through the combination of images with information, through the deep embedding of each image in a software program like Google Earth with layers of data. This move, widely associated with what Tim O'Reilly calls "Web 2.0" approaches to data production, management, and interfaces, radically shifts the relationship between images and their readability and cultural function. Now each image is a data layer and, perhaps, not even a very important data layer. At the same time, software like Google Earth demonstrates Katherine Hayles's arguments about contemporary information logics of pattern and randomness and the ways in which meanings flicker past and away from us just as they come into signification.[25]

But what stands out about these virtual windows and their views goes back to McLuhan and his idea—his fear even—that electronic technologies were cutting us off from ourselves, making us "numb" to our own bodies and immediate surroundings just as we connected remotely to new vistas. There is something immensely powerful in using Google Earth that is simultaneous with and connected to its interface's relative transparency and ease of use. Intuitively I explore oceanographic landscapes and leap off-planet for a trip around the Moon, albeit without Georges Méliès's quaint Moon creatures accompanying me.

Instead of reenacting Méliès's *Trip to the Moon* (1902), I am like a far more recent hero known for his travel off-planet— Superman. Those who are familiar with his stories know that when Superman has a problem or some real thinking to do, there is only one place to go—the Fortress of Solitude. But when Superman wants to blow off steam, to joyride, or, as in the first *Superman* film (Donner, 1978), change the course of history just to save his girl, he goes to outer space and tools around. In the films and comics, these trips visually demonstrate Superman's vast power and alien superiority—he can orbit Earth with ease, spin it on its axis, float and breathe in space.

But what if everyone is a superman or superwoman? And each of us is virtually spinning and manipulating our planet like so many pixels? I am not and don't want to be a paranoid outmoded technophobe here, but instead I want to call attention to the responsibilities we bring with us into virtual spaces where we can easily fly, zoom, or build worlds. Nor am I necessarily calling for limits to access to these tools—instead I want to open up a discussion about what these new tools and their vistas make possible. What happens when our virtual windows open up vistas so vast that everyone has virtual superpowers (of vision, of mastery over the Earth)? Who then, is Clark Kent? As the evil baddie Syndrome in *The Incredibles* (Bird, 2004) puts it, "Once everyone's super, no one will be."

This book then, has sought to deflate the overblown rhetoric and ahistorical comparisons between old and new through its examination of television technologies, computer peripherals, video game systems, comic books, television series, advertising, and the other ephemera that are part and parcel of media culture. Yet, here at the end, the question about how television invented new media has been both answered and, in some sense, evaded. Perhaps this is because the question should not be about how television invented new media but why the logics of invention, mediation, and novelty are so pervasive.

On the Matter
of Invention

> Everyone always wants new things. Every-
> body likes new inventions, new technology.
> People will not be replaced by machines.
> In the end life and business are about
> human connections. And computers are
> about trying to murder you in a lake. And to
> me the choice is easy.
>
> —Michael Scott, *The Office*

WHAT IS INVENTION, ANYWAY? Often it speaks
of a certain kind of history or a certain approach to storytelling: great achievements that push forward the human race to
some yet-unknown horizon of expectations. It's easy to picture
a stereotypical "inventor" type of person, taught to us from
comic books, movies, television. He (somehow the mad scientist inventor tends to be a man) looks a lot like Dr. Horrible,
surrounded by lab equipment, his hair tousled by his intellectual
labor and the dirty, sweaty work of making something new.
This book began with the premise that it would tell how television (an abstract thing, a technology, a set of industries, various
media forms) invented new media (an abstract thing, a technology, a set of industries, various media forms). What it does
toward this is demonstrate the many ways that television and
new media are joined technologically and culturally—in devices,
in formats, in experiences. But ultimately, television cannot be
credited with inventing new media, since it is not one thing.

Bill Gates invented BASIC for the Altair, Steve Wozniak invented the Apple (and the *Breakout* game, let's not forget that), Tim Berners-Lee invented HTML, Shawn Fanning invented Napster—but none of these things can possibly encompass all that is "new media." What's more, by creating systems for sharing information, code, and culture, invention has become a more diffuse and collaborative effort these days. It is increasingly difficult to be a lone genius. Instead, teams invent operating systems and new video games, just as teams invent and make movies like *Avatar* (and its software and hardware) happen. It is simply more convenient to say that one person (James Cameron) "invented" it, but that person is just a node in a larger structure, even if that person is a very noisy node clamoring for lots of credit. But that's new media for you: lots of incompatible perspectives, simultaneously pronouncing their views. It's a bit like a global Twitter feed.

Perhaps that is why many people approach new media like the hapless, do-gooder, bumbling boss of *The Office* (2005–present), Michael Scott (Steve Carrell).[1] False dichotomies between humans and machines or old technology and new technology fundamentally mistake new media as having an "either/or" logic. It doesn't. As *How Television Invented New Media* has shown, the emergence and rise of new media is understood, accompanied by, and in conversation with the media that preceded and often launches it. Novelty may be charming, but at the end of the day, which screen are you looking at and what's on it?[2]

"CAN YOU HEAR ME NOW?": PASSING THE FUTURE BY

Writing about the present is a losing proposition. So is writing about a decentralized set of computer networks or about the abstract and concrete ways television signifies culturally, or even writing about the fluid and unfixed objects of the digital era, which are, in essence, never stable or complete but always in flux and "under construction" as pieces of code existing on a server somewhere. And yet, we must seek to understand the present, computer networks, television, and the digital, or else we undermine the very cultures we help to create and occupy. One must contemplate and behold these unfixed and shifting representations, both in the tradition of the great "beholders" of art and "spectators" of cinema, as well as in and on their own terms, seeing both the data and the cultures they depict.

There is a touching passage of images and words that plays toward the end of Chris Marker's 1982 essay film, *Sans Soleil.* Marker's female narrator reads a letter from the "camera man" about his travels, as Marker's strange travelogue imagery floats by. She reads: "I remember January in Tokyo, or rather I remember the images that I filmed in January in Tokyo. They have put themselves in the place of my memory, they are my memory. I ask myself how people remember if they do not make movies, or photographs, or tapes, how mankind used to go about remembering."

Marker's meditation upon memory sticks with me—sticks, in fact, to my ribs. I ache when I hear it intoned in the film, a sad comment toward the end of an essay about the very impossibility of memory or records to capture the past and present as the flit by us. I return to it, again and again. I wonder, what will future cultures make of the exhausting explorations of self-portraiture brought about by the social networking era? Will they see how we struggled to create versions of ourselves through images, sounds, "walls" of content, software, collections of arbitrary data meaningful only to their collectors? Will they find our virtual architectures in ruins? As data lost in formats that no longer exist (who makes tapes anymore?)?

I write this at a time when I, like Marker, should be in Tokyo but I am not: fear of a global flu pandemic has kept me home. Months of online research into which Tokyo neighborhoods I would have visited have now been shelved: this accumulated data was virtual tourism for a virtual era. The human body—and its ability to transport and transmit infection—is still a fragile "meat" bag, as the cyberpunks once called it. Yet, I virtually explore "kawaii" culture and superflat art of a nation that has been a driving force for popular culture, animation, and gaming for years. *Hello Kitty*, are you out there? Would you like to be my friend on Facebook?

The argument that television "invented" new media is not immediately apparent at first glance. In fact, as television's cultural status continues to be widely perceived as part of low, popular culture, contending that television is central to new media also means contending with the cultural and intellectual baggage associated with television. This is what I call the "I don't watch television" syndrome, most commonly suffered by somewhat pretentious liberal intellectuals who see television as beneath their attention (see chapter 2). Too bad for them—they are missing out on some of the most important and far-reaching media content that has been made during the past sixty years or so. Writing about how television invented new media is at once a nostalgic and futuristic enterprise, a bit like watching *The Jetsons* (1962–1963) in 2010 on a flat-screen TV. In 1962, the ABC prime-time situation comedy *The Jetsons* prognosticated how a family in the future might live: the robot maid, automated walkways, personal flying vehicles were shown alongside the "normal" problems of 1960s suburban life, like an obnoxious boss, nosy neighbors, teenage daughters and their hysterias. Watching *The Jetsons* in 2010 means looking back and forward simultaneously at a future once imagined in and by the past. There is some distortion in the translation of one medium into another, some "stretching" of the image's aspect ratio as it is transported to its place on the contemporary view screen. Through the combination of television with new media, we have imagined futures, built actual technologies and generated complex new forms of media production and reception, all at once. Our memories are, like Marker's narrator puts it, overtaken by the images we have seen, as well as by the tools we have used to see them.

RETRONYM: AN ANALOG
FUTURE-HISTORY

There is another phrase from Marker's film I like: "Who remembers all that? History throws its empty bottles out the window." Marker's claim here—about how history discards its detritus, throwing its "empty bottles" out the window like some hungover drunk—is one that new media studies can learn from as it endeavors to grow as an academic field or intersection of fields. We need to remember "all that" as we boldly examine just what makes today's new media so different (so exciting).

Sometimes I think that the academic disregard for popular media like television and video games bespeaks more than simply an ingrained hierarchy of objects and knowledges that places TV and games beneath notice. Instead, it strikes me that television and video games—and computer software and networks—are exceedingly difficult objects to apprehend in a scholarly fashion. Furthermore, as objects studied in relatively new disciplines, television, video games, and computers are still objects approached from a range of methodologies. There is no one way to "read" a video game or perform an analysis of social network. These new objects require new skills and new kinds of academics.

If it seems odd and self-serving to close a book about how *television* invented new media by invoking a 1982 film by a relatively obscure experimental French filmmaker—known to most people solely because Terry Gilliam remade his nearly still short film *La Jetée* (Marker, 1962) into *Twelve Monkeys* (1995)—then that's just the point. While cultural elites, subcultures, and low cultures still thrive and intermingle and inform each other today (as the art critic Clement Greenberg put it, one cannot have the avant-garde without the rear-garde), it is through their mutual contagion—their transport and transmission—that new forms emerge and ideas spread.[3] Such contagions and contaminations of high by low and the reverse of that, too, is something that new media, through networks, users, software, and connectivity, excels at and makes increasingly easy to do.

Despite the anxieties and concerns of a television industry very much in crisis over and about the medium's relationship to "new media," I am not worried.[4] Nor do I worry that television will be subsumed by new media and then churned out as an unrecognizable post-convergence form. No, instead, I just sit back on my sofa and watch the widescreen, digital television with my digital video remote in one hand and my laptop at the ready should I want to quickly look up an actor, writer, or producer while in front of my set. I think it is clear that television will keep on inventing new media for many years to come, just as new media will forge on and create more possibilities for interactivity and simulation that will surely influence how we use, imagine, and approach this productive medium in the years to come. We shall have to recycle and refashion history's bottles as they lie in shards beneath our windows.

APPENDIX A: VIDEO GAME
AND DIGITAL SOURCES

VIDEO GAMES

Asteroids, Atari, 1979

Basketball, Atari, 1978

Brain Age, Nintendo, 2006

Breakout, Atari, 1976

Dance, Dance Revolution, Konami, 1998

Diablo, Blizzard Entertainment, 1997

Doom, id Software, 1993

Final Fantasy, Square, 1987

Final Fantasy X, Square, 2002

Grand Theft Auto, Rockstar North, 1997

Grand Theft Auto 3, Rockstar North and Rockstar Vienna, 2001

Grand Theft Auto: Vice City, Rockstar North and Rockstar Vienna, 2002

Guitar Hero, Harmonix Music Systems, 2006

Halo: Combat Evolved, Gearbox Software and Bungee Studios, 2002

Halo 2, Bungee Studios, 2004

Home Run, Atari, 1978

Katamari Damacy, Namco Bandai, 2004

Kingdom Hearts, Square, 2002

The Lord of the Rings: The Fellowship of the Ring, Pocket Studios, Surreal Software, and WXP, 2002

Pac-Man, Namco Bandai, 1979

Pong, Atari, 1972

Quake, id Software, 1996

Rock Band, Harmonix Music Systems, 2007

Space Invaders, Taito, 1978

StarCraft, Blizzard Entertainment, 1998
Tennis for Two, William Higginbotham, 1958
Tony Hawk's Pro Skater, Neversoft Entertainment, Treyarch,
    Natsume, Edge of Reality, and Activision, 1999
Tony Hawk's Pro Skater 3, Neversoft Entertainment, Vicarious
    Visions, HotGen, and Sheba Games, 2001
Wolfenstein 3D, id Software, 1992
World of Warcraft, Blizzard Entertainment, 2004
World of Warcraft: The Burning Crusade, Blizzard Entertainment,
    2007
World of Warcraft: Wrath of the Lich King, Blizzard Entertain-
    ment, 2007

DIGITAL SOURCES

Apple, http://www.apple.com.
Apple-History.com, http://apple-history.com.
The Bronze Beta, http://www.bronzebeta.com/.
Channels.com, http://www.channels.com/.
Dr Horrible's Sing-Along Blog, http://drhorrible.com/.
The Extratextuals, http://www.extratextual.tv/.
Funny or Die, http://www.funnyordie.com.
Hulu, http://www.hulu.com.
Intellivision, http://www.intellivisiongames.com.
Just TV, http://justtv.wordpress.com/.
MIT Convergence Culture Consortium, http://www.convergence
    culture.org/.
Red versus Blue, http://redvsblue.com/home.php.
"Resident Evil Dance Party," *YouTube,* http://www.youtube.
    com/watch?v=3MHS7e8cmqM.
"South Park Digital Studios Press Release," http://www.south
    parkstudios.com/news/3405, 25 March 2008.
"Timeline of Computing 1950–1979." *Wikipedia,* http://
    en.wikipedia.org/wiki/Timeline_of_computing_1950–
    1979.
Whedonesque.com, http://www.whedonesque.com.
Where is Raed?, http://dear_raed.blogspot.com/.
"WoW—The Internet is for PORN!," *YouTube,* http://www.
    youtube.com/watch?v=zN7LZ499aQc.
YouTube, http://www.youtube.com.

Appendix B: Relevant Film and Television Sources

Films

Being There, Hal Ashby, 1979
eXistenZ, David Cronenberg, 1999
Ghost in the Shell, Mamoru Oshii, 1995
The Matrix, Andy and Lana Wachowski, 1999
Pleasantville, Gary Ross, 1998
Stay Tuned, Peter Hyams, 1992
Tron, Steven Lisberger, 1982
Videodrome, David Cronenberg, 1983

Television

Alias, ABC, 2001–2006
All in the Family, CBS, 1971–1979
Arrested Development, FOX, 2003–2006
Battlestar Galactica, Sci-Fi Channel, 2004–2009
The Big Bang Theory, CBS, 2008–present
The Bionic Woman, ABC, 1976–1977 and NBC, 1977–1978
Buffy the Vampire Slayer, The WB, 1997–2001 and UPN,
   2001–2003
Entourage, HBO, 2004–present
Freakylinks, FOX, 2000–2001
Gilmore Girls, The WB, 2000–2006 and The CW,
   2006–2007
How I Met Your Mother, CBS, 2005–present
The Incredible Hulk, CBS, 1978–1982
Lost, ABC, 2004–2010
The Middleman, ABC Family, 2008
The Office, NBC, 2005–present

Roots, ABC, 1977
South Park, Comedy Central, 1997–present
The Six Million Dollar Man, ABC, 1974–1978
Veronica Mars, UPN, 2004–2006 and The CW, 2006–2007
The West Wing, NBC, 1999–2006

Notes

Acknowledgments

1. This acknowledgments section is admittedly inspired by the opening to the Rhona Berenstein's excellent book *Attack of the Leading Ladies: Gender, Sexuality, and Spectatorship in Classic Horror Cinema* and its eloquent metacritique of how we acknowledge those who fortify us in our efforts.

Introduction

1. For more on the false opposition between old and new media see Caldwell, "The Business of New Media."
2. A good example of such promotional synergy between divisions was in evidence on the 2 December 2009 airing of the Fox series *Bones* (2005–present). In this episode, "The Gamer in the Grease," multiple characters camped out in line in order to attend the opening screening of the Fox film *Avatar* (Cameron, 2009). This promotional synergy was even more intertextual and tongue-in-check as the actor Joel Moore, who plays a recurring character on *Bones*, waited in line to attend a film in which he costars—in *Avatar* Moore plays the scientist, Na'vi sympathizer, and "dreamwalker" Norm Spellman. More traditional spot advertisements and trailers for *Avatar* were also shown during the commercial breaks for *Bones*.
3. For the sake of readability I have transposed the *Oxford English Dictionary* entry, which reads: "A system for reproducing an actual or recorded scene at a distance on a screen by radio transmission, usu. with appropriate sounds; the vision of distant objects obtained thus." "Television," *Oxford English Dictionary*, 2nd ed. (Oxford: Oxford University Press, 1989).
4. In Peter Weir's *The Truman Show*, a film that is highly critical of television's invasive and constant presence in its viewers' lives and imaginations, daydreamer Truman Burbank (Jim Carrey), who is unaware that his actions are filmed and broadcast, poignantly reenacts the moon landing by drawing an astronaut's suit around his face in the mirror. Remarkably, Truman's suit also appears like a

1950s-era television receiver with antennae. Both his performance of the moon landing and its doubling as a television set encapsulating Truman's head, as well as the audience's knowledge that this moment is being broadcast, locate Truman in the center of his own imaginary television screen as star of the show.

5. Of course this image also has a classic mise-en-abyme structure: with one's computer displaying a computer displaying a sky referencing René Magritte's painting.

6. Sterling's description of the everyday technologies that so occupied cyberpunk writers was taken up by Henry Jenkins, Tara McPherson, and Jane Shattuc as the title for their introduction, "The Culture That Sticks to Your Skin: A Manifesto for a New Cultural Studies," in *Hop on Pop: The Politics and Pleasures of Popular Culture* (3–25).

7. The soft contact lens will be saved for another book on cyborgian bodily amendments.

8. Although digital, online media certainly bears some resemblance to both radio and film, it is television's combination of radio broadcasting technologies and genres with the cathode ray screen that situates TV technology as the more direct forebear to the personal computer technologies that followed it. Personal computers, of course, eventually combined such digital elements as hard drives, computer processors, and computer networking capabilities with CRT screens and sound input/output components, along with borrowing the keyboard technology of the typewriter.

9. See Lynn Spigel, *Make Room for TV* (1992) and *Welcome to the Dreamhouse* (2001), as well as Karal Ann Marling's *As Seen on TV: The Visual Culture of Everyday Life in the 1950s* (1994).

10. In this instance, as in many others today, the computer screen becomes a virtual television set for viewing media streamed from the internet or played from a DVD or other source.

11. Indeed, see Edward Castronova's work on the virtual economies and cultures of *World of Warcraft* and other massively multiplayer games in *Synthetic Worlds: The Business and Culture of Online Games* (2005), and Celia Pearce's book on gamer communities, *Communities of Play: Emergent Cultures in Multiplayer Games and Virtual Worlds* (2009).

12. Although digital humanities resonates with new media studies and new media studies can be understood as a subset of digital humanities, these are distinct approaches. Digital humanities emerged out of the need to bring humanities scholarship into contact with new digital tools and approaches, whereas new media studies often takes as its subjects the software and hardware used in a digital humanities approach.

13. Bolter and Grusin go so far as to claim that "virtual reality functions for its contemporary user as the so-called cinema of attractions did for filmgoers at the turn of the century" (254).

14. See Lisa Cartwright, "Film and the Digital in Visual Studies: Film Studies in the Era of Convergence" (2002), and Barbara Klinger, *Beyond the Multiplex: Cinema, New Technologies and the Home* (2006).

15. See Timothy Druckrey, *Electronic Culture: Technology and Visual Representation (1996)*; Mark Dery, *Flame Wars: The Discourse of Cyberculture (1994)*; Lynn Cherny and Elizabeth Reba Weise, *Wired Women (1996)*; Chris Hables Gray, *The Cyborg Handbook (1995)*; and David Bell and Barbara Kennedy, *The Cybercultures Reader (2000)* as examples.

16. See George Landow's work that juxtaposed hypertext and critical theory, especially *Hypertext: The Convergence of Contemporary Critical Theory and Technology* (1992) and *Hyper/Text/Theory* (1994).

17. See John Caldwell, *Production Culture: Industrial Reflexivity and Critical Practice in Film and Television* (2008).

18. Although 1993 might seem like an arbitrary date for the history of this field, it is a strategic one. Arguably, "cybercultural studies" was extremely subcultural prior to 1993, when the *South Atlantic Quarterly* published its groundbreaking "flame wars" issue. The World Wide Web had existed for just one year in 1993 and was still primarily used by academic specialists. But by this time, work on new media was beginning to circulate more broadly within academia. Another key early anthology, *Cyberspace: First Steps*, edited by Michael Benedikt, was published by MIT Press in 1991. Other existing academic tomes on new media that had been released by the early 1990s include Arthur Kroker and Michael A. Weinstein, *Data Trash: Theory of the Virtual Class* (1994); Mark Poster, *The Mode of Information: Poststructuralism and Social Context* (1990); and Donna Haraway, *Simians, Cyborgs, and Women: The Reinvention of Nature* (1991). Notably, the online journal *Postmodern Culture*, which does not overtly take new media as its content but has always been published as a new media text, began publication in 1990 with an issue that included Andrew Ross's essay on the politics of hacking, "Hacking Away at the Counterculture."

19. See Carolyn Marvin, *When Old Technologies Were New: Thinking about Electric Communication in the Late Nineteenth Century* (1988), and Wendy Hui Kyong Chun and Thomas Keenan, eds., *New Media and Old Media: A History and Theory Reader* (2006), especially Chun's introduction, "Did Somebody Say New Media?" 1–13.

20. It is actually a prairie dog and not a chipmunk in the video. For an explanation and examples of the Internet memes seen in the Weezer video, see NME.com's "Weezer's 'Pork and Beans': A YouTube Guide," http://www.nme.com/blog/index.php?blog=10&p=3659&more=1&c=1&tb=1&pb=1.

21. Video game scholar Jesper Juul's work is central to the theories of ludology in video game studies. See *Half-Real: Video Games between Real Rules and Fictional Worlds* (2005). Also see Jan Simons, "Narrative, Games, and Theory" (2007).

22. See Sobchack, *Carnal Thoughts: Embodiment and Moving Image Culture* (2004), as well as Murray, *Hamlet on the Holodeck: The Future of Narrative in Cyberspace* (1998).
23. Steve Jones discusses *Halo* and its use of an expanded narrative universe including alternate reality games in *The Meaning of Video Games: Gaming and Textual Strategies* (2008).
24. The previously mentioned volume *Cyberspace: First Steps* is particularly useful in this regard, as its authors primarily imagine "cyberspace" as virtual reality systems.
25. The years 2008 and 2009 have seen the rise of real-time microblogging via software like Twitter and Facebook, both constructed so I can readily let my 205 "friends" know that "Sheila is making dinner." This obsessive chronicling of the everyday picks up earlier online diary and image trends such as webcams. See my essay, "Lurking and Looking: Webcams and the Construction of Cybervisuality" (2000).
26. McLuhan is often accused of being a technological determinist in his approach to media, yet despite his tendency to link technologies directly to cultural change, his attention to *how* media inflects the everyday is still quite useful.
27. Such an approach to media's "dailyness" is not, in fact, new. See Paddy Scannell, *Radio, Television and Modern Life: A Phenomenological Approach* (1996), which analyzes time and the Heideggerian "dasein" to understand radio's unique production of dailyness. Also cultural studies scholarship on the everyday ways fans and consumers use media is instructive here, as is the work of film scholar Vivian Sobchack and philosopher Elizabeth Grosz, each of whom contends with the time, space, and experience of everyday acts such as movie going or encountering architecture from the "outside."
28. Jake Coyle, "*Funny or Die* Leaps to TV in New HBO series" (2010).
29. See John Caldwell, "The Business of New Media" (2002).
30. The Iraqi blog "Where Is Raed?" is a good demonstration of the virtual convergence of geographies, first-person narrative, and global literacies. Written during the 2003 U.S. invasion and occupation of Iraq by Salam al-Janabi under the pseudonym Salam Pax (respectively, the Arabic and Latin words for "peace"), the blog was widely read around the globe and later lead to a book, *Salam Pax: The Baghdad Blog* (2003).
31. See Murphy, "Converging Channels (of Discourse): Linking between Televisual and Digital Networks" (2001).
32. Chun explains how TCP/IP works at various points in *Control and Freedom*, especially 63–65.
33. See MIT's Convergence Culture Consortium or the blogs of media scholars such as the collaboratively authored blog *The Extratextuals* (http://www.extratextual.tv/) or Jason Mittell's *Just TV* (http://justtv.wordpress.com/).

34. See Winston, *Media Technology and Society, A History: From the Telegraph to the Internet* (1998).

35. It would be nice to see Baudrillard's use of the term "code" as a prefiguration of his later interest in the virtual or in computers, but it is far more likely he is invoking code in a semiotic sense, as fits with his biography and with the academic fashions of the 1970s.

36. Although video game and computer games are quite separate forms, I will largely refer to both as "video games" to avoid confusion and go along with industry norms. I will only single out a game as a computer game when it is relevant to an argument or to point out the use of a rhetorical strategy, as in the case of Atari games produced for Atari "computer systems" rather than an Atari "video game system," as console systems like Atari's 2600 model later came to be called.

CHAPTER 1 "THIS IS INTELLIGENT TELEVISION"

1. See Raymond Williams on "flow" as an ideological and aesthetic structure often conflated with the medium of television in *Television: Technology and Cultural Form* (1975). For televisual flow and new media, see Richard Dienst, *Still Life in Real Time* (1994).

2. Even the spate of high-tech superhero/super-science programs of the 1970s (including *The Incredible Hulk*, *The Six Million Dollar Man*, and *The Bionic Woman*) did not domesticate computers but kept these new tools safely within high-tech laboratory settings.

3. For more on 1970s television, see Kirsten Lentz, "Quality vs. Relevance: Feminism, Race, and the Politics of the Sign in 1970s Television," *Camera Obscura* (2000). For the "vast wasteland" speech, see Erik Barnouw, *Tube of Plenty* (1990), 300–301.

4. Of course, Willy Higinbotham's early oscilloscope game might also be framed as a "divergence" from the technology's intended purpose. See Leonard Herman, *Phoenix: The Fall and Rise of Home Videogames* (1994), for more on Higinbotham.

5. So this isn't *actually* a simultaneous convergence; instead, the television becomes a multipurpose—we might even say multimedia—technology.

6. As the *StarCraft* (1998) professional competitions in South Korea show, video games also have audiences who watch a player or players interact with the game directly. Their experiences should not be discounted, but are outside the scope of this essay.

7. I am grateful to Andrew Covert for his astute comments on the switch between technological functions.

8. While gaming violence is not my focus, surely it is arguable that violence is more widely readable than the more nuanced aspects of video games, which are rarely commented upon in mainstream, alarmist coverage of gaming.

9. This approach also follows Johnson's argument in *Everything Bad Is Good for You*, in which he argues that much of the most widely disregarded popular forms (television, video games, etc.) require high-level cognitive processing. Such engagements with media are often overlooked amid the critique of media content.

10. See Fredric Jameson, *Postmodernism; or, The Cultural Logic of Late Capitalism and Other Essays* (1991), and Stephen Paul Miller, *The Seventies Now: Culture as Surveillance* (1999) on, respectively, postmodern aesthetics and 1970s popular culture. See also René Moreau, *The Computer Comes of Age: The People, the Hardware, and the Software* (1984).

11. See Roy A. Allan's *A History of the Personal Computer: The People and the Technology* (2001).

12. Brian Winston refers to Atari's 1970s and early 1980s gaming systems as "low-level home computers" in *Media Technology and Society* (1998), 232.

13. Most home gaming systems can be hooked up to a video projector or larger screen device using adapters, but they are marketed primarily toward a home user, and it is assumed that gamers will be playing on television screens. Recent systems, like Microsoft's Xbox 360, are even calibrated to work best with high-definition television sets. Some third-party manufacturers have sold larger gaming screens and low-end projectors with limited success.

14. This feminization of the television appliance is aptly noted in Lynn Spigel, *Make Room for TV* (1992); Spigel and Denise Mann, eds., *Private Screenings: Television and the Female Consumer* (1992); and Karal Ann Marling, *As Seen on TV: The Visual Culture of Everyday Life in the 1950s* (1994).

15. By describing the postwar popularity and widespread acceptance of television as a cultural installation, I hope to mark this historical moment as one where televisual technology was, for the first time, widely available and quickly adopted by consumers as a new mass medium. "Installation" is a term commonly used to describe how domestic appliances are put into living spaces, by either a specialist or the consumer.

16. For both amateur and professional scholars, there is some dispute over whether or not Higinbotham's oscilloscope game "counts" as the first video game or is an early predecessor to the genre. See Mark J. P. Wolf, *The Medium of the Video Game* (2001), xi.

17. Of course, successful game play and interactivity depend on the combination of one's watching with one's playing. Both modes of reception are present and depend upon one another.

18. Jeffrey Sconce describes how television was mystified during the 1960s in his analysis of *The Outer Limits* in "'The Outer Limits' of Oblivion" (1997).

19. For more on how early viewers related to television technology, see ibid.

20. Also see the Wikipedia entry on the history of computing. "Timeline of Computing 1950–1979." http://en.wikipedia.org/wiki/Timeline_of_computing_1950–1979.

21. Charles Bernstein makes a similar argument about the nonutility of video games in his essay "Play It Again, Pac-Man," which originally appeared in *Postmodern Culture* 2, 1 (September 1991). The essay was later reprinted in Mark J. P. Wolf, ed., *The Medium of the Video Game* (2001).

22. This historical grouping of games via the "generation" of their hardware holds sway in the industry, though largely in inaccurate ways, as often new releases are labeled, sometimes years in advance, as "next generation" systems.

23. This negotiation of framing games as toys or computers would continue, as Nintendo's breakthrough Nintendo Entertainment System would prove. The NES was explicitly marketed as a toy, with a pack-in Robot Operating Buddy (R.O.B.), because video game systems had, by then, a poor reputation.

24. See also http://www.intellivisiongames.com.

25. Today, of course, one can purchase a computer that has been designed primarily for gaming, such as the systems made by Alienware. Here gaming also functions as the machine's primary purpose, but these systems are still functionally PCs first, gaming computers second, unlike most of the systems I am discussing here. That is, one doesn't turn the machine's defaults into a game mode. Instead one encounters a PC operating system and then "switches" the machine into game mode.

26. Though, as Mark J. P. Wolf has reminded me, the televisual aspect ratio was initially inherited from film's early aspect ratio.

27. See various scholars on home theater discourse; in particular, see Barbara Klinger, "The New Media Aristocrats: Home Theater and the Domestic Film Experience" (1998).

28. Although I don't have the space to engage in a full literature review of television studies here, relevant texts include Spigel's *Make Room For TV*; the *Channels of Discourse* anthologies edited by Robert Clyde Allen (1987, 1992); Anna McCarthy's *Ambient Television: Visual Culture and Public Space* (2001); and work by William Boddy, Jeffrey Sconce, Heather Hendershot, Bambi Haggins, Susan Douglas, and others. The anthology *Television Studies*, edited by Toby Miller (2002) is a good overview of issues in the field.

29. See Henry Jenkins, *Fans, Bloggers, and Gamers* (2006).

CHAPTER 2   IS THIS CONVERGENCE?

1. Later in the chapter, I will discuss machinima in more detail, but briefly, the term refers to "machine cinema" made by capturing explicitly "performed" footage from a computer game and then editing that footage together with its own soundtrack. Machinima is

a fan and gamer practice that is at odds with the copyright ownership of the game software by its producers and distributors.

2. To "pwn" in gamer discourse is based on a mistyping of "own" as in
"I owned you during that game." To be pwned is to be thoroughly
beaten or humiliated by an opponent. Spelling of this slang word
can vary.

3. See the lengthy interview with the South Park Studios animators by
the staff of Machinima.com: "'Make Love, Not Warcraft': An Interview with Frank Agnone, J. J. Franzen, and Eric Stough" (2006).

4. *South Park*'s intentionally crude visual style is a running joke in
the series, for the construction paper cut-out style is achieved via
high-end computers and software programs (initially the series used
supercomputers but has used Apple computers and products in
recent seasons). Dustin Driver, "South Park Studios: No Walk in the
Park," *Apple Professional Profiles*, 2009, http://www.apple.com/pro/
profiles/southpark/index.html. Actual cut-out construction paper
was only used for the unaired series pilot, which can be seen on the
South Park Studios Web site. TeamSpeak software uses VOIP (voice
over IP) technology to allow multiple users to communicate in a
designated chat channel. It has been widely adopted by computer
gamers to use while playing MMORPGs like *World of Warcraft*.

5. Since 2006, other series have exploited the foibles and style of
MMORPGs, specifically in the CBS series *The Big Bang Theory*
(2008–present), which aired the gaming addiction–themed episode
"The Barbarian Sublimation," set partially in the game *Age of Conan*
(2008), in October 2008. The CBS dramatic series *NCIS* (2003–
present) aired "The Immortals" about MMORPG gaming on a
naval aircraft carrier in October 2003, but massively multiplayer
games are still rarely the primary narrative element on American
network television.

6. See "Make Love, Not Warcraft."

7. One common genre of machinima is the music video, in which
a group of characters dance and sing in coordination with one
another to a specific song that is later added to the footage.
See "WoW—The Internet Is for Porn," http://www.youtube.
com/watch?v=zN7LZ499aQc&feature=PlayList&p=B3066AA77
E1C17F2&playnext=1&playnext_from=PL&index=8, or "Resident Evil Dance Party," http://www.myoelectric.net/. Perhaps one
of the most well-known machinima series is *Red vs. Blue*, which
uses footage from the science-fiction action series *Halo* to create a
character-driven series. See Rooster Teeth Productions, http://
redvsblue.com/home.php.

8. See Brian Szabelski, "Toyota, *World of Warcraft* Come Together in
New Tacoma Ad" (2007).

9. See "Make Love, Not Warcraft."

10. It is worth noting that there have been many less successful narrative
attempts to "converge" new media forms with television—one key

early effort was the Fox series *Freakylinks* (2000–2001), which had a narrative centered on the production of a Web site that was available to fans as though created by characters within the show's diegetic world. Yet this "linked" show did not succeed in the ratings and was pulled by the network midway into its first season.

11. See "South Park Digital Studios Press Release" (2008).
12. The South Park Digital Studios games are mostly variations on classic arcade and video games, so that *South Park Ass Kicker* (2007) is actually a parody of *Mortal Kombat* (1992).
13. The animation features go into great detail and use sophisticated production terms when describing how shots were conceived and then mapped out and achieved using different software programs.
14. This slogan was one of ABCFamily's network taglines during summer 2008 on-air promotions.
15. Javier Grillo-Marxuach, personal conversation with the author, February 2008.
16. This change of ethnicity came at the direction of network executives. Javier Grillo-Marxuach, personal conversation with the author, May 2009.
17. This is the type of convergence discussed by Henry Jenkins in "Searching for the Origami Unicorn: *The Matrix* and Transmedia Storytelling" (2006). Jenkins does not label this "iconographic convergence" as I have, but instead discusses transmedia storytelling. Iconographic convergence more precisely describes what content is reworked, translated, and converged across media, whereas storytelling is part of what changes with each shift of media format. Iconographic, visual elements typically provide continuity across media formats, whereas storytelling strategies often shift.
18. Perhaps this is why television producers now routinely dedicate preproduction time into developing transmedia elements for network series. In 2009, Javier Grillo-Marxuach began developing transmedia elements for NBC's miniseries *Day One* (2010).
19. See Danah Boyd on the "networked publics" of social networking sites: "Why Youth Heart Social Networking: The Role of Networked Publics in Teenage Social Life" (2008).
20. This short essay appears in *Cinema Journal* 45, 1 (Fall 2005). Caldwell expands upon his argument in *Production Culture: Industrial Reflexivity and Critical Practice in Film and Television* (2008).
21. The term "paratext" is taken from the work of literary theorist Gérard Genette, who argues for the study of seemingly peripheral textual elements like accompanying illustrations or titles when analyzing a text. Various film and media scholars have adapted Genette's ideas to media texts. See *Paratexts: Thresholds of Interpretation* (1997).
22. See Alex Ebel, "Welcome to MILF Island: Authorial Sitcoms in the Postnetwork Era" (2008).
23. Pruitt's "fairy tale," posted online, is particularly interesting. It is a "tell-all" backstage story by a disgruntled, recently fired employee

that is told using recognizable "characters" representing Whedon and the series's star, Sarah Michelle Gellar. Pruitt's online post, "The Parable of the Knight" is (still) often referred to as "Pruittgate" in online forums and significantly shaped the discourse of *The Bronze*, one of the earliest and most populous *Buffy* forums often visited by *Buffy* producers, writers, and actors while the show was in production. Pruitt's post has been removed online, but the controversy can be followed through the Bronze Beta Archive: http://www.bronze-beta.com/. Mark Andrejevic's analysis of television fan site Television without Pity is a thoroughgoing piece on online fan forums: "Watching *Television Without Pity*: The Productivity of Online Fans" (2008).

24. For more on contemporary fan practices, see Jonathan Gray, Cornell Sandvoss, and Lee Harrington, eds., *Fandom: Identities and Communities in a Mediated World* (2007).

25. Arguably, a fan who watches a show and follows it online via character blogs, spoiler sites, industry news columns, and so on, is watching a very different program from that watched by a viewer who just tunes in for an episode.

26. In a 21 May 2009 interview, television writer/producer Javier Grillo-Marxuach discussed the "transmedia" focus of contemporary network series with me, including the *Lost* ARG. Prior to even shooting a series pilot, Marxuach and other writers and producers are now hired to develop convergence/transmedia content as an inherent part of a prospective series' narrative world.

27. David Bianculi, "Mitchell Hurwitz Discusses His Show *Arrested Development*" (2005).

28. Whedonesque.com is a blog maintained by Whedon aficionados online. I am using the term here to also denote stylistic elements associated with Whedon-produced media.

29. Goodman, "Some Things Just Deserve a List of Their Own" (2008).

30. Film essayist Eric Faden uses the term "absorb" to describe how film, television, and new media "convergences" quickly become understood under the logic of the more dominant media, usually film. See "The Cyberfilm: Hollywood and Computer Technology" (2001).

CHAPTER 3   FROM TUBE TO A "SERIES OF TUBES"

1. For instance, there is no technological reason why a Web site should be divided into "channels"—yet users are familiar with the notion of the channel from television discourse, so here the television terminology allows for a bridge between a new mode and old, while at the same time it can also block off new paradigms for ordering and organizing information that speak more fully to how the new technology differs from the old. Channels.com is an video information

aggregator online and many video or entertainment sites use this model, such as YouTube.com, where user-generated "channels" are also organized into a channel directory by genre, user, aim of work (political, as produced by a business partner of YouTube, etc.).

2. Indeed, television is actually many languages at once, as it exists as a global satellite technology utilized in many regions throughout the world. Here I am referring, however, to the technological stylistic "language" that is mostly closely associated with American commercial television, a dominant "dialect" of television that can be understood easily and is recognizable.

3. On 28 June 2006, in Senate hearings on communications reform, Senator Stevens remarked: "The Internet is not something you just dump something on. It's not a truck. It's a series of tubes. And if you don't understand those tubes can be filled and if they are filled, when you put your message in, it gets in line and it's going to be delayed by anyone that puts into that tube enormous amounts of material, enormous amounts of material."

4. I have been unable to locate academic sources on the Macintosh TV, so my material here comes from primary sources like the Apple corporate support site and Apple fan-produced online texts, including Apple-History.com and Wikipedia (en.wikipedia.org).

5. Various EyeTV devices work as broadcast, cable, satellite, or high-definition television tuners via FireWire or USB connections to the computer. Elgato produces both the EyeTV software and hardware.

6. For a concise critique and overview of cultural studies methods and approaches, including analysis of the "cultural dopes" debates, see Meaghan Morris, "Banality in Cultural Studies" (1988).

7. See Sheila C. Murphy, *Lurking and Looking: Media Technologies and Cultural Convergences of Spectatorship, Surveillance, and Voyeurism* (2002).

8. For more on timeshifting, see Paul Virilio, "The Third Window" (1988).

9. In 1932, Aldous Huxley described the society of the future as one where "at the foot of every bed . . . was a television box" (*Brave New World* 234).

10. For more on global media events, see Marshall McLuhan, *Understanding Media* (1994); Daniel Dayan and Elihu Katz, *Media Events: The Live Broadcasting of History* (1992).

11. See Lawrence Lessig, *Code and Other Laws of Cyberspace* (1999). Also see Lessig's popular Weblog, *LessigBlog*: www.lessig.org/blog/.

12. Although there are certainly exceptions to this division between visual studies and media archaeology, interdisciplinary visual studies scholars tend to compare various forms of visuality in their work, often not drawing great attention to differences in form and medium, while media archaeologists are primarily concerned with medium specificity.

13. Chun's two major film examples, *The Matrix* (Wachowski and Wachowski, 1999) and *Ghost in the Shell* (Oshii, 1995), are presented via ideological analysis and narrative analysis with reference to the science fiction literature of William Gibson and others; both could benefit from the tools of film theory, especially apparatus theory and a discussion of film imagery.

14. Lynn Spigel, "Television's Next Season?" (2005).

15. For more on the multiplication of screens via electronic media and the use of window as a technological metaphor, see Friedberg, *The Virtual Window: From Alberti to Microsoft* (2006).

16. See David Julyk, "'The Trouble with Machines Is People': The Computer as Icon in Post-War American Culture, 1946–1970" (2008).

17. Of course, technological improvements and developments have led to increasingly larger TV screens over the years.

18. For more on televisual formats and modes, see Nick Browne, "The Political Economy of the Television (Super) Text" (1994), and also Raymond Williams, *Television: Technology and Cultural Form* (1974).

19. Jane Feuer's essay on liveness has been central to discussions of liveness that have continued on in television and media studies since it was published in 1983. See Feuer, "The Concept of Live TV" (1983). Jeffrey Sconce discusses the category of liveness of electronic media in *Haunted Media: Electronic Presence from Telegraphy to Television,* (2000). Sconce uses liveness to understand how technologies become humanized or, in the case of telegraphy, spiritualized. Mary Ann Doane describes television's temporality through the categories of information, crisis, and catastrophe. Television has, according to Doane, an "insistent presentness"—a category in which time is presented as perpetually in-the-now. See Doane, "Information, Crisis, Catastrophe" (1990).

20. As in Don DeLillo's novel *White Noise* (1986).

21. In my digital media theory course, I ask students to go a day without their digital technologies, and most find that they miss not only their on-demand media player personal soundtrack but also miss its physical weight and presence as they walk around campus.

22. For more on this, see Browne, "The Political Economy of the Television (Super) Text." Note that the television schedule is synchronized to the twenty-four-hour day; film historians have commented on how the railroad standardized this clock and time in the late nineteenth century. See Lynne Kirby, *Parallel Tracks: The Railroad and Silent Cinema* (1997).

23. See Heather Hendershot, *Saturday Morning Censors: Television Regulation before the V-Chip* (1998), especially chapter 1.

24. Although this may seem ambitious, it is not uncommon. A close friend of mine who is an engineer routinely opens up his television set to dust inside it, to adjust picture quality, or check cable and plug connections. The steady success of the Radio Shack chain of home

electronics stores testifies to the popularity of tinkering with home technologies such as television, cable, and telephones.

25. See Cristina Gena, "Designing TV Viewer Stereotypes for an Electronic Program Guide" (2001) for more on how programmers approach and design guides with viewers in mind. Also see Michael Ehrmantraut et al., "The Personal Electronic Program Guide—Towards the Pre-selection of Individual TV Programs" (1996), which describes methods and approaches for organizing and filtering program data for the new era of digital and interactive television.

26. The full Internet address for the coverage of this suit is http://news.com.com/2100–1023–933398.html?tag=rn. See also Jennifer Lee, "Technology: Digital Video Recorders; First, Replay TV 4000 Must Face the Courts" (2001).

27. For an extended discussion of how digital video recorders are caught up in the rhetoric of liveness, as well as discussions of content browsing and the erosion of a national television audience, see William Boddy, "Redefining the Home Screen: The Case of the Digital Video Recorder" in *New Media and Popular Imagination* (2004), 100–107.

CHAPTER 4   ALT-CTR

1. What counts as a video game is, of course, widely debated. See Mark J. P. Wolf, "The Video Game as Medium," in *The Medium of the Video Game,* ed. Mark J. P. Wolf (2001), 13–34.

2. See the research of NPD Group for 2008: http://www.npd.com/press/releases/press_090202.html.

3. Mickey Meece, "Inspiration Can Be Found in Many Places but You Have to Be Looking for It" (October 2008), B9.

4. Of course, one of the major skeptical arguments against video games as a social force is that games are too immersive for gamers, who, once they are involved in the pull of a game's interactive and stereotypically violent narrative action, are unable to discern between the world of the game and reality outside of the game. Athough I am arguing that games do in fact "leak" out into the nongame Real, the way in which they do so is fundamentally different from the stereotype of a gamer getting lost in the unreal and becoming a "lone gunman."

5. Although only some video games overtly address the gamer's body, nearly all games require the sophisticated manipulation of controller buttons, often at high speeds and timed precisely. Even those denigrated as "button-mashing" games still necessitate motor control and eye-hand coordination.

6. See Nicholas Negroponte, *Being Digital* (1995), and Esther Dyson, George Gilder, George Keyworth, and Alvin Toffler, "Cyberspace and the American Dream: A Magna Carta for the Knowledge

Age" (1994). Their description of cyberspace includes: "unlimited knowledge, decentralized, moving in space, a vast array of owner-ships, empowerment, hospitable if you customize it, flow, float, and fine-tune," among other criteria.

7. Vivian Sobchack eloquently theorizes the synaesthia of spectator-ship and hand/eye connections in her essay, "What My Fingers Knew: The Cinesthetic Subject, or Vision in the Flesh," in *Carnal Thoughts: Embodiment and Moving Image Culture* (2004), 53–84.

8. See Julian Dibbell, *My Tiny Life: Crime and Passion in a Virtual World* (1998).

9. Cinematics, so called because they remediate film sequences, are typically a reward for successful play. Some game franchises, in particular the *Final Fantasy* and *Metal Gear Solid* games, have an extremely high cinematic-to-game play ratio. Yet it is not uncom-mon for gamers to disrupt or bypass cinematic sequences if a game will allow one to do so.

10. The inaugural first person shooter was *Wolfenstein 3D* in 1992; *Doom* was released later that year. In 1996, *Quake* was the first 3D FPS.

11. Here Manovich is critiquing the notion of interactivity, since users typically interact through and with software that was designed by someone else. Yet I wonder if identifying with others, such as soft-ware designers, is necessarily a bad thing. Claims like this set the stage for software/code studies, which prioritize more "pure" forms of interaction directly with computer languages and codes.

12. For definitions of these terms, see the Videogames.com Web dic-tionary, "Defining Video Games": http://www.videogames.com/features/universal/defining_games/p9_02.html.

13. *GTA: Vice City* (2002) made the Lion and the Lamb Project's "Dirty Dozen" of dangerous toys for 2002–2003, along with five other video games, even though it is rated M for mature (voluntary rat-ing) and ostensibly not marketed to children. Early exceptions that are critical studies of video games are: Mark J. P. Wolf, *The Medium of the Video Game* (2001); Justine Cassell and Henry Jenkins, eds., *From Barbie to Mortal Kombat: Gender and Computer Games* (1998); and Marsha Kinder, *Playing with Power in Movies, Television, and Video Games: From Muppet Babies to Teenage Mutant Ninja Turtles* (1991).

14. There are also numerous third-party input devices available for home gaming systems, such as light guns, steering wheels and pedals, fishing reels, and so on.

15. See: http://www.nintendo.com/systems/n64/n64_acc_rumbler.jsp.

16. For example, "Let's Do This Together Now!" is one of the repeated refrains from an exercise game in the *Wii Fit* program, encourag-ing the gamer to "box" against a virtual training bag. Offscreen, the gamer holds the Wii-mote controls and quickly jabs and uppercuts along with the encouragement offered by the offscreen boxing coach. http://www.xbox.com/.

17. Scott Bukatman's key volume on *Terminal Identity: The Virtual Subject in Postmodern Science Fiction* (1993) theorizes how subjectivity is formed in front of the computer screen or terminal. The embodied computer "terminal identity" experiences Bukatman describes offer interesting parallels to video games, which often are situated within science fiction frameworks.

18. The cottage industries dedicated to the proliferation of products designed to control and wrangle cables, as well as "decorative" power strips and designer "skins" to dress up technologies, are all indications of how new media has become familiar and incorporated into the home and are seen as a reflection of the user's sense of personal taste.

CONCLUSION

1. Similar ventures include: Sony Ericsson z55 phone in development, which silences calls or alarms when the user waves his or hand over the handset; GestureTek's Airpoint remote bar with two cameras—users can operate Powerpoint by waving their hands at the remote bar; 3V Systems infrared ZCam that translates small hand gestures into onscreen movement. Kim Ryan, "With Just a Wave of Your Hand," *San Francisco Chronicle*, 21 January 2008.

2. In the press and corporate Web documents about Reactrix, Inc., it is unclear what those "over 100 million impressions" are, precisely—100 million glimpses? Eyeballs? Time-based engagement with the material? One assumes this is a measure of some physiological attention paid to the system, though how this measure is taken is unclear.

3. Takahashi, "Reactrix Puts You in the Picture" (2004).

4. One can easily find videos of the Reactrix system at work on either the corporate Web site (www.reactrix.com) or via a Web search engine. My favorite example is of a Jack Russell terrier chasing down an interactive ball, barking in excitement as he wins the game with the system.

5. Ryan, "With Just a Wave of Your Hand." There are similar software applications for Apple's iPhone that allow users to feed fish, pop bubble wrap, or just experience the pleasures of touching the screen.

6. See André Bazin, *What Is Cinema?* (2004), and J. David Bolter and Richard A. Grusin, *Remediation: Understanding New Media* (1999).

7. I would be remiss not to note Anne Friedberg's treatise on the shared spaces and uses of malls and multiplexes, *Window Shopping: Cinema and the Postmodern Condition* (1994).

8. Abbey Klaassen, "CEO Rewrites Branded-Entertainment Script to Include 'People Placement'" (2005).

9. Later Burnett goes on to claim, "No technology has had a greater influence on this unfolding history of images than television" (*How Images Think* 2).

10. Written by Trey Parker, airdate 7 November 2007.

11. Vaporware is a software industry term used to describe code that has been promised but not delivered, so that all of its abilities are vapor. Jeffrey Sconce reworked the term to apply to new media theory, comparing such work with eighteenth-century Dutch tulipomania in his essay "Tulip Theory" (2003).

12. McGhee, "Preface," to *Here Is Television, Your Window to the World* by Thomas Hutchinson (1946), v–vii.

13. Michael Benedikt, "Cyberspace: Some Proposals," in *Cyberspace: First Steps*, ed. Michael Benedikt (1991), 119–224.

14. See s.v. "Google Earth" on Wikipedia: http://en.wikipedia.org/wiki/Google_earth.

15. http://earth.google.com/intl/en/.

16. Anne Friedberg, *The Virtual Window: From Alberti to Microsoft* (2006).

17. One reason for this understanding of all geographical user interfaces (GUIs) as Windows can be found in the history of GUIs, in which multiple individuals and corporations, including Apple Computer and Microsoft, looked to a GUI prototype developed at Xerox Parc. See *The Encyclopedia of New Media: An Essential Reference to Communication and Technology*, ed. Steven E. Jones (Thousand Oaks: Sage, 2003). 18. Windows on the World was also the name of the renowned restaurant at the top of the World Trade Center, which operated from 1976 until its destruction in 2001. My use of the phrase "windows on the world" here is taken not from the restaurant but from Thomas Hutchinson's 1946 book, *Here Is Television: Your Window to the World*. The restaurant, of course, also literalized the metaphoric and economic rhetoric of the "window on the world" concept through its architectural position and panoramic setting atop the global economic marketplace of the World Trade Center.

19. "About 'Today'" (2010).

20. Ibid.

21. The adage that pornography drives technological progress is a widely accepted belief among longtime Internet users and network engineers who have witnessed the Internet shift from a text-only social space to a media-rich environment. Jonathan Coopersmith, among others, has traced out some of the connections between the dissemination of pornography and the development of new technologies in his work, especially "Pornography, Technology, and Progress," ICON 4 (1998), 94–125.

22. See Marshall McLuhan, *The Gutenberg Galaxy: The Making of Typographic Man* (1962).

23. See also Eric McLuhan, "The Source of the Term 'Global Village'" (1996).
24. Marshall McLuhan, "The Medium Is the Message," reprinted in *The New Media Reader*, ed. Noah Wardrip-Fruin and Nick Montfort (2003), 203–209.
25. See N. Katherine Hayles, "Virtual Bodies and Flickering Signifiers," in *How We Became Posthuman: Virtual Bodies in Cybernetics, Literature, and Informatics* (1999).

EPILOGUE

1. In this episode (6 August 2008), Michael is angry because he is being forced to use new computer technologies at work (Powerpoint and the new corporate Web site) and, in an attempt to prove his embrace of new technology, he incorrectly follows the advice from a GPS unit and drives his car into a lake.
2. Perhaps another good question to ask is, "Does it bother you that you are ending your day looking at a screen?" But that's another book entirely.
3. Such a move is in keeping with the methodological paradigm of visual studies and the field's imperative to examine a broader and more diverse spectrum of visual cultures.
4. John Caldwell performs an especially useful analysis of the old media versus new media industry debates in his essay "The Business of New Media" (2002).

Bibliography

"About 'Today.'" *MSNBC Interactive*. 3 March 2010. http://today.msnbc. msn.com/id/3079108/ns/today/.

Allan, Roy A. *A History of the Personal Computer: The People and the Technology*. London, Ont.: Allan Publishers, 2001.

Allen, Robert Clyde, ed. *Channels of Discourse: Television and Contemporary Criticism*. London: Methuen, 1987.

———. *Channels of Discourse, Reassembled: Television and Contemporary Criticism*. 2nd ed. Chapel Hill: University of North Carolina Press, 1992.

Andrejevic, Mark. "Watching *Television without Pity:* The Productivity of Online Fans." *Television and New Media* 9, 1 (2008): 24–46.

Barnouw, Erik. *Tube of Plenty: The Evolution of American Television*. 2nd rev. ed. New York: Oxford University Press, 1990.

Baudrillard, Jean. "Requiem for the Media." In *The New Media Reader*, ed. Noah Wardrip-Fruin and Nick Montfort. Cambridge: MIT Press, 2003. 278–288.

Bazin, André. *What Is Cinema?* Berkeley: University of California Press, 2004.

Bell, David, and Barbara M. Kennedy. *The Cybercultures Reader*. London: Routledge, 2000.

Bellamy, Robert, and James Walker. *Television and the Remote Control: Grazing on a Vast Wasteland*. New York: Guilford Press, 1996.

Benedikt, Michael, ed. *Cyberspace: First Steps*. Cambridge: MIT Press, 1991.

Berenstein, Rhona J. *Attack of the Leading Ladies: Gender, Sexuality, and Spectatorship in Classic Horror Cinema*. New York: Columbia University Press, 1996.

Berger, John. *Ways of Seeing*. London: Penguin, 1972.

Bernstein, Charles. "Play It Again, Pac-Man." *Postmodern Culture* 2, 1 (1991). Reprinted in *The Medium of the Video Game*, ed. Mark J. P. Wolf. Austin: University of Texas Press, 2002. 155–168.

Bianculli, David. "Mitchel Hurwitz Discusses His Show *Arrested Development*." *Fresh Air*. Recorded 3 November 2005.

Boddy, William. *New Media and Popular Imagination: Launching Radio, Television, and Digital Media in the United States*. Oxford: Oxford University Press, 2004.

———. "Redefining the Home Screen: Technological Convergence as Trauma and Business Plan." In *Rethinking Media Change: The Aesthetics of Transition*, ed. David Thorburn, Henry Jenkins, and Brad Seawell. Cambridge: MIT Press, 2003. 191–202.

Bogost, Ian. *Unit Operations: An Approach to Videogame Criticism*. Cambridge: MIT Press, 2006.

Bolter, J. David, and Richard A. Grusin. *Remediation: Understanding New Media*. Cambridge: MIT Press, 1999.

Bowman, Lisa M. "Suit Filed over Replaytv Features." 2002. *CNET News*, 6 June 2002. http://news.cnet.com/Suit-filed-over-ReplayTV-features/2100-1023_3-933398.html?tag=mncol.

Boyd, Danah. "Why Youth Heart Social Networking: The Role of Networked Publics in Teenage Social Life." *Macarthur Foundation Series on Digital Media and Learning—Youth, Identity, and Digital Media* (2008): 119–142.

Browne, Nick. "The Political Economy of the Television (Super) Text." In *American Television: New Directions in History and Theory*. Langhorne, Pa.: Harwood Academic Publishers, 1994. 69–79.

Bukatman, Scott. *Terminal Identity: The Virtual Subject in Postmodern Science Fiction*. Durham: Duke University Press, 1993.

Burnett, Ron. *How Images Think*. Cambridge: MIT Press, 2004.

Caldwell, John. "The Business of New Media." In *The New Media Book*, ed. Dan Harries. London: BFI, 2002. 55–68.

———. *Electronic Media and Technoculture*. New Brunswick: Rutgers University Press, 2000.

———. *Production Culture: Industrial Reflexivity and Critical Practice in Film and Television*. Durham: Duke University Press, 2008.

———. "Welcome to the Viral Future of Cinema (Television)." *Cinema Journal* 45, 1 (Fall 2005): 90–97.

Cartwright, Lisa. "Film and the Digital in Visual Studies: Film Studies in the Era of Convergence." *Journal of Visual Culture* 1, 1 (2002): 7–23.

Cassell, Justine, and Henry Jenkins, eds. *From Barbie to Mortal Kombat: Gender and Computer Games*. Cambridge: MIT Press, 1998.

Castronova, Edward. *Synthetic Worlds: The Business and Culture of Online Games*. Chicago: University of Chicago Press, 2005.

Cherny, Lynn, and Elizabeth Reba Weise. *Wired Women: Gender and New Realities in Cyberspace*. Seattle: Seal Press, 1996.

Chun, Wendy Hui-Kyong. *Control and Freedom: Power and Paranoia in the Age of Fiber Optics*. Cambridge: MIT Press, 2006.

————. "Did Somebody Say New Media?" In *New Media, Old Media: A History and Theory Reader*. ed. Wendy Hui Kyong Chun and Thomas Keenan. New York: Routledge, 2006. 1–13.

Chun, Wendy Hui Kyong, and Thomas Keenan, eds. *New Media, Old Media: A History and Theory Reader*. New York: Routledge, 2006.

Coopersmith, Jonathan. "Pornography, Technology, and Progress." *ICON* 4 (1998), 94–125.

Coupland, Douglas. *Generation X: Tales for an Accelerated Culture*. New York: St. Martin's, 1991.

Coyle, Jake. "*Funny or Die* Leaps to TV in New HBO Series." *ABC News/Technology*. 17 February 2010. http://abcnews.go.com/Technology/wireStory?id=9865648.

Dayan, Daniel, and Elihu Katz. *Media Events: The Live Broadcasting of History*. Cambridge: Harvard University Press, 1992.

DeLillo, Don. *White Noise*. New York: Penguin Books, 1986.

DeMaria, Rusel, and Johnny L. Wilson. *High Score!: The Illustrated History of Electronic Games*. New York: McGraw-Hill/Osborne, 2003.

Dery, Mark. *Flame Wars: The Discourse of Cyberculture*. Durham: Duke University Press, 1994.

Dibbell, Julian. *My Tiny Life: Crime and Passion in a Virtual World*. New York: Holt, 1998.

Dienst, Richard. *Still Life in Real Time: Theory after Television*. Durham: Duke University Press, 1994.

Doane, Mary Ann. "Information, Crisis, Catastrophe." In *Logics of Television: Essays in Cultural Criticism*, ed. Patricia Mellencamp. Bloomington: Indiana University Press, 1990. 222–239.

Druckrey, Timothy. *Electronic Culture: Technology and Visual Representation*. New York: Aperture, 1996.

Dyson, Esther, George Gilder, George Keyworth, and Alvin Toffler. "Cyberspace and the American Dream: A Magna Carta for the Knowledge Age." Progress and Freedom Foundation, release 1.2 (22 August 1994). http://www.pff.org/issues-pubs/futureinsights/fi1.2magnacarta.html.

Ebel, Alex. "Welcome to MILF Island: Authorial Sitcoms in the Postnetwork Era." Undergraduate honors thesis, University of Michigan, 2008.

Ehrmantraut, Michael, et al. "The Personal Electronic Program Guide—Towards the Pre-Selection of Individual TV Programs." Paper prepared for the ACM Conference on Information and Knowledge Management. Rockville, Md.: 12–16 November 1996.

Enzensberger, Hans Magnus. "Constituents of a Theory of the Media." In *The New Media Reader*, ed. Noah Wardrip-Fruin and Nick Montfort. Cambridge: MIT Press, 2003. 261–275.

Faden, Eric. "The Cyberfilm: Hollywood and Computer Technology." *Strategies* 14, 1 (2001): 77–90.

Feuer, Jane. "The Concept of Live TV." In *Regarding Television: Critical Approaches—an Anthology*, ed. E. Ann Kaplan. Frederick, Md.: University Publications of America, 1983. 12–22.

Flanagan, Mary. "Mobile Identities, Digital Stars, and Post-Cinematic Selves." *Wide Angle* 21, 1 (1999): 77–93.

Friedberg, Anne. *The Virtual Window: From Alberti to Microsoft*. Cambridge: MIT Press, 2006.

———. *Window Shopping: Cinema and the Postmodern Condition*. Berkeley: University of California Press, 1993.

Gauntlett, David. *Web.Studies: Rewiring Media Studies for the Digital Age*. London: Arnold, 2000.

Gena, Christina. "Designing TV Viewer Stereotypes for an Electronic Program Guide." *Lecture Notes in Computer Science* 2109/2009. Berlin/Heidelberg: Springer, 2001. 274–276.

Genette, Gérard. *Paratexts: Thresholds of Interpretation*. Cambridge: Cambridge University Press, 1997.

Gibson, William. *Neuromancer*. New York: Ace Books, 2000.

Goodman, Tim. "Some Things Just Deserve a List of Their Own." *San Francisco Chronicle*, 26 December 2008, E1.

Gray, Chris Hables. *The Cyborg Handbook*. New York: Routledge, 1995.

Gray, Jonathan, Cornel Sandvoss, and C. Lee Harrington. *Fandom: Identities and Communities in a Mediated World*. New York: NYU Press, 2007.

Greenberg, Clement. "Avant-Garde and Kitsch." In *Clement Greenberg: The Collected Essays and Criticism*, ed. John O'Brian. Chicago: University of Chicago Press, 1986. 5–21.

Grosz, E. A. *Architecture from the Outside: Essays on Virtual and Real Space*. Cambridge: MIT Press, 2001.

Guins, Raiford. "'Intruder Alert! Intruder Alert!' Video Games in Space." *Journal of Visual Culture* 3, 2 (2004): 195–211.

Hanson, Christopher. "The Instant Replay: Time and Time Again." *Spectator* 28, 2 (2008): 51–60.

Haraway, Donna. *Simians, Cyborgs, and Women: The Reinvention of Nature*. New York: Routledge, 1991.

Harries, Dan. *The New Media Book*. London: BFI, 2002.

Hayles, N. Katherine. *How We Became Posthuman: Virtual Bodies in Cybernetics, Literature, and Informatics*. Chicago: University of Chicago Press, 1999.

Helfand, Jessica. *Screen: Essays on Graphic Design, New Media, and Visual Culture*. New York: Princeton Architectural Press, 2001.

Herman, Leonard. *Phoenix: The Fall and Rise of Home Videogames*. Union, N.J.: Rolenta Press, 1994.

Hendershot, Heather. *Saturday Morning Censors: Television Regulation before the V-Chip*. Durham: Duke University Press, 1998.

Hutchinson, Thomas H. *Here Is Television, Your Window to the World*. New York: Hastings House, 1946.

Huxley, Aldous. *Brave New World*. Reprint, New York: Perennial Classics, 1998.

Ihde, Don. *Bodies in Technology*. Minneapolis: University of Minnesota Press, 2002.

Jameson, Fredric. *Postmodernism; or, The Cultural Logic of Late Capitalism and Other Essays*. Durham: Duke University Press, 1991.

Jenkins, Henry. *Convergence Culture: Where Old and New Media Collide*. New York: NYU Press, 2006.

———. *Fans, Bloggers, and Gamers: Exploring Participatory Culture*. New York: NYU Press, 2006.

———. "Pop Cosmopolitanism: Mapping Cultural Flows in an Age of Media Convergence." In *Fans, Bloggers, and Gamers: Exploring Participatory Culture*. New York: NYU Press, 2006. 152–172.

———. "Searching for the Origami Unicorn: The Matrix and Transmedia Storytelling." In *Convergence Culture: Where Old and New Media Collide*. New York: NYU Press, 2006. 93–130.

Jenkins, Henry, Tara McPherson, and Jane Shattuc, eds. *Hop on Pop: The Politics and Pleasures of Popular Culture*. Durham: Duke University Press, 2002.

Johnson, Steven. *Everything Bad Is Good for You: How Today's Popular Culture Is Actually Making Us Smarter*. New York: Riverhead Books, 2006.

Jones, Steve, ed. *The Encyclopedia of New Media: An Essential Reference to Communication and Technology*. Thousand Oaks: Sage, 2003.

Jones, Steven E. *The Meaning of Video Games: Gaming and Textual Strategies*. New York: Routledge, 2008.

Julyk, David P. "'The Trouble with Machines Is People.' The Computer as Icon in Post-War America: 1946–1970." Ph.D. dissertation, University of Michigan, 2008.

Juul, Jesper. *A Casual Revolution: Reinventing Video Games and Their Players*. Cambridge: MIT Press, 2009.

———. *Half-Real: Video Games between Real Rules and Fictional Worlds*. Cambridge: MIT Press, 2005.

Kent, Steve L. *The Ultimate History of Video Games: From Pong to Pokémon and Beyond: The Story Behind the Craze That Touched Our Lives and Changed the World*. Roseville, Cal.: Prima, 2001.

Kilday, Gregg. "AFI Picks 'Moments of Significance.'" 28 December 2008. *HollywoodReporter.com*. http://www.hollywoodreporter.com/.

Kinder, Marsha. *Playing with Power in Movies, Television, and Video Games: From Muppet Babies to Teenage Mutant Ninja Turtles*. Berkeley: University of California Press, 1991.

Kirby, Lynne. *Parallel Tracks: The Railroad and Silent Cinema.* Durham: Duke University Press, 1997.

Kittler, Friedrich, Dorthea von Mücke, and Philippe L. Similon. "Gramophone, Film, Typewriter." *October* 41 (Summer 1987): 101–118.

Klaassen, Abbey. "CEO Rewrites Branded-Entertainment Script to Include 'People Placement.'" *Advertising Age,* 5 December 2005: 76.

Klinger, Barbara. *Beyond the Multiplex: Cinema, New Technologies, and the Home.* Berkeley: University of California Press, 2006.

———. "The New Media Aristocrats: Home Theater and the Domestic Film Experience." *The Velvet Light Trap* (Fall 1998): 4–19.

Kosinski, Jerzy. *Being There.* New York: Harcourt Brace Jovanovich, 1971.

Kroker, Arthur, and Michael A. Weinstein. *Data Trash: The Theory of the Virtual Class.* New York: St. Martin's, 1994.

Landow, George P. *Hyper/Text/Theory.* Baltimore: Johns Hopkins University Press, 1994.

———. *Hypertext: The Convergence of Contemporary Critical Theory and Technology.* Baltimore: Johns Hopkins University Press, 1992.

Lee, Jennifer. "Technology: Digital Video Recorders; First, Replay TV 4000 Must Face the Courts." *New York Times,* 31 December 2001, C3.

Lentz, Kirsten Marthe. "Quality versus Relevance: Feminism, Race, and the Politics of the Sign in 1970s Television." *Camera Obscura* (2000): 45–93.

Lessig, Lawrence. *Code and Other Laws of Cyberspace.* New York: Basic Books, 1999.

Lotz, Amanda D. *The Television Will Be Revolutionized.* New York: NYU Press, 2007.

Lupton, Deborah. "The Embodied Computer/User." *Body & Society* 1 (1995): 97–112.

"'Make Love, Not Warcraft': Q&A with Frank Agnone, J. J. Franzen, and Eric Stough." *Machinima.com,* 15 November 2006. http://www.machinima.com/article/view&id=459.

Manovich, Lev. *The Language of New Media.* Cambridge: MIT Press, 2001.

Marling, Karal Ann. *As Seen on TV: The Visual Culture of Everyday Life in the 1950s.* Cambridge: Harvard University Press, 1994.

Marvin, Carolyn. *When Old Technologies Were New: Thinking about Electric Communication in the Late Nineteenth Century.* New York: Oxford University Press, 1988.

McCarthy, Anna. *Ambient Television: Visual Culture and Public Space.* Durham: Duke University Press, 2001.

McLuhan, Eric. "The Source of the Term 'Global Village.'" *McLuhan Studies* 1, 2 (1996). http://www.chass.utoronto.ca/mcluhan-studies/v1_iss2/1_2art2.htm.

McLuhan, Marshall. *The Gutenberg Galaxy: The Making of Typographic Man.* Toronto: University of Toronto Press, 1962.

———. "The Medium Is the Message." In *The New Media Reader,* ed. Noah Wardrip-Fruin and Nick Montfort. Cambridge: MIT Press, 2003. 203–209.

———. *Understanding Media: The Extensions of Man.* Cambridge: MIT Press, 1994.

McPherson, Tara. "Self, Other and Electronic Media." In *The New Media Book,* ed. Dan Harries. London: BFI, 2002. 183–194.

Meece, Mickey. "Inspiration Can Be Found in Many Places but You Have to Be Looking for It." *New York Times,* 23 October 2008, B9.

Mellencamp, Patricia, ed. *Logics of Television: Essays in Cultural Criticism.* Bloomington: Indiana University Press, 1990.

Miller, Stephen Paul. *The Seventies Now: Culture as Surveillance.* Durham: Duke University Press, 1999.

Miller, Toby, ed. *Television Studies.* London: BFI, 2002.

Moreau, René. *The Computer Comes of Age: The People, the Hardware, and the Software.* Cambridge: MIT Press, 1984.

Morris, Meaghan. "Banality in Cultural Studies." *Discourse* 10, 2 (Spring/ Summer 1988): 2–29.

Murphy, Sheila C. "Converging Channels (of Discourse): Linking between Televisual and Digital Networks." *Strategies: A Journal of Theory, Culture and Politics* 14, 1 (May 2001): 139–147.

———. *Lurking and Looking: Media Technologies and Cultural Convergences of Spectatorship, Surveillance, and Voyeurism.* Ann Arbor: UMI Press, 2002.

———. "Lurking and Looking: Webcams and the Construction of Cybervisuality." In *Moving Images: From Edison to the Webcam,* ed. John Fullerton and Astrid Söderbergh-Widding. Sydney, Australia: John Libbey, 2000. 173–180.

———. "'This is Intelligent Television': Early Video Games, TV and the Emergence of the Personal Computer." *The Video Game Theory Reader 2.* Eds. Mark Wolf and Bernard Perron, Routledge, 2008. 197–212.

Murray, Janet Horowitz. *Hamlet on the Holodeck: The Future of Narrative in Cyberspace.* Cambridge: MIT Press, 1998.

Nakamura, Lisa. "Race in/for Cyberspace." In *Reading Digital Culture,* ed. David Trend. Malden, Mass.: Blackwell, 2001. 226–235.

Negroponte, Nicholas. *Being Digital.* New York: Knopf, 1995.

Nelson, Jenny. "The Dislocation of Time: A Phenomenology of Television Reruns." *Quarterly Review of Film and Video* 12, 3 (1990): 79–92.

Orwell, George, Thomas Pynchon, and Erich Fromm. *Nineteen Eighty-Four: A Novel.* New York: Plume, 2003.

Pavlik, John V., and Shawn McIntosh. *Converging Media: An Introduction to Mass Communication.* Boston: Pearson, Allyn and Bacon, 2004.

Pax, Salam. *Salam Pax: The Baghdad Blog.* London: Guardian Books, 2003.

Pearce, Celia. *Communities of Play: Emergent Cultures in Multiplayer Games and Virtual Worlds.* Cambridge: MIT Press, 2009.

Perron, Bernard, and Mark J. P. Wolf, eds. *The Video Game Theory Reader 2.* New York: Routledge, 2009.

Poster, Mark. *The Mode of Information: Poststructuralism and Social Context.* Chicago: University of Chicago Press, 1990.

Riley, David. "2008 Video Game Software Sales across Top Global Markets Experience Double-Digit Growth" (2009). *The NPD Group.* http://www.npd.com/press/releases/press_090202.html.

Ross, Andrew. "Hacking Away at the Counterculture." *Postmodern Culture* 1, 1 (1990), unpaginated.

Ryan, Kim. "With Just a Wave of Your Hand." *San Francisco Chronicle,* 21 January 2008, D1.

Scannell, Paddy. *Radio, Television, and Modern Life: A Phenomenological Approach.* Cambridge, Mass.: Blackwell, 1996.

Sconce, Jeffrey. *Haunted Media: Electronic Presence from Telegraphy to Television.* Durham: Duke University Press, 2000.

———. "The 'Outer Limits' of Oblivion." In *The Revolution Wasn't Televised: Sixties Television and Social Conflict,* ed. Lynn Spigel and Michael Curtin. New York: Routledge, 1997. 21–46.

———. "Tulip Theory." In *New Media: Theories and Practices of Digitextuality,* ed. Anna Everett and John Thornton Caldwell. New York: Routledge, 2003. 179–193.

Simons, Jan. "Narrative, Games, and Theory." *Game Studies* 7, 1 (2007). http://gamestudies.org/0701/articles/simons.

Sobchack, Vivian. *Carnal Thoughts: Embodiment and Moving Image Culture.* Berkeley: University of California Press, 2004.

———. "The Scene of the Screen: Envisioning Photographic, Cinematic, and Electronic 'Presence.'" In *Materialities of Communication,* ed. Hans Ulrich Gumbrecht and Karl Ludwig Pfeiffer. Stanford: Stanford University Press, 1994. 83–106.

"South Park Digital Studios Press Release." *South Park Studios,* 25 March 2008. http://www.southparkstudios.com/news/3405.

Spigel, Lynn. *Make Room for TV: Television and the Family Ideal in Postwar America.* Chicago: University of Chicago Press, 1992.

———. "Television's Next Season?" *Cinema Journal* 45, 1 (Fall 2005): 83–90.

———. *Welcome to the Dreamhouse : Popular Media and Postwar Suburbs.* Durham: Duke University Press, 2001.

Spigel, Lynn, and Denise Mann. *Private Screenings: Television and the Female Consumer.* Minneapolis: University of Minnesota Press, 1992.

Standage, Tom. *The Victorian Internet: The Remarkable Story of the Telegraph and the Nineteenth-Century's On-Line Pioneers.* New York: Walker, 1998.

Sterling, Bruce. *Mirrorshades: The Cyberpunk Anthology.* New York: Arbor House, 1986.

Stone, Allucquère Rosanne. *The War of Desire and Technology at the Close of the Mechanical Age.* Cambridge: MIT Press, 1995.

————. "Will the Real Body Please Stand Up? Boundary Stories about Virtual Cultures." In *Cyberspace: First Steps,* ed. Michael Benedikt. Cambridge: MIT Press, 1991. 81–118.

Szabelski, Brian. "Toyota, *World of Warcraft* Come Together in New Tacoma Ad," 6 October 2007. http://blogcritics.org/gaming/article/toyota-world-of-warcraft-come-together/.

Takahashi, Dean. "Reactrix Puts You in the Picture." *San Jose Mercury News,* 30 December 2004, Business section.

Thorburn, David, Henry Jenkins, and Brad Seawell, eds. *Rethinking Media Change: The Aesthetics of Transition.* Cambridge: MIT Press, 2003.

Trend, David. *Reading Digital Culture.* Malden, Mass.: Blackwell, 2001.

Turkle, Sherry. *Life on the Screen: Identity in the Age of the Internet.* New York: Simon & Schuster, 1995.

Uricchio, William. "Historicizing Media in Transition." In *Rethinking Media Change: The Aesthetics of Transition,* ed. David Thorburn, Henry Jenkins, and Brad Seawell. Cambridge: MIT Press, 2003. 23–38.

————. "Television's Next Generation: Technology/Interface Culture/ Flow." In *Television after TV: Essays on a Medium in Transition,* ed. Lynn Spigel and Jan Olsson. Durham: Duke University Press, 2004. 163–182.

Virilio, Paul. "The Third Window." *Global Television,* ed. Cynthia Schneider and Brian Wallis. Cambridge: MIT Press, and New York: Wedge, 1988. 185–198.

Virilio, Paul, and Julie Rose. *Open Sky.* London: Verso, 1997.

Wardrip-Fruin, Noah, and Pat Harrigan, eds. *Second Person: Role-Playing and Story in Games and Playable Media.* Cambridge: MIT Press, 2007.

Wardrip-Fruin, Noah, and Nick Montfort, eds. *The New Media Reader.* Cambridge: MIT Press, 2003.

Watson, Mary Ann. *Defining Visions: Television and the American Experience in the Twentieth Century.* London: Blackwell, 2008.

Whitney, Daisy. "Whedon Says It's All About the Message, Not the Medium; Daisy's Digital Diary." *TelevisionWeek* 27 (14 September 2008): 15.

Williams, Linda, ed. *Viewing Positions: Ways of Seeing Film.* New Brunswick: Rutgers University Press, 1995.

Williams, Raymond. *Television: Technology and Cultural Form.* London: Fontana, 1974.

178 *Bibliography*

Winston, Brian. *Media Technology and Society, A History: From the Telegraph to the Internet.* London: Routledge, 1998.

Wolf, Mark J. P., ed. *The Medium of the Video Game.* Austin: University of Texas Press, 2001.

Wolf, Mark J. P., and Bernard Perron, eds. *The Video Game Theory Reader.* New York: Routledge, 2003.

———. *The Video Game Theory Reader 2.* New York: Routledge, 2009.

Zielinski, Siegfried. *Audiovisions: Cinema and Television as Entr'actes in History.* Amsterdam: Amsterdam University Press, 1999.

INDEX

About the Author

Sheila C. Murphy is an assistant professor in the Department of Screen Arts and Cultures at the University of Michigan, where she teaches about digital media theory, video games and culture, and the history of emerging technologies. Her research interests range from the visual culture of computer interfaces to the identity politics of online subcultures. Even though she is often online and can be reached electronically at scmurphy@umich.edu, she still enjoys watching television on a TV without timeshifting.